Advanced Work-based Practice in the Early Years

CW01081308

Inspired by the first-hand experiences of those studying early childhood education and care, this book supports students as they gain advanced knowledge and skills, and embark on the journey from inexperienced student to graduate professional.

Bringing together advanced theory, links to research, and illustrative case studies, *Advanced Work-based Practice in the Early Years* enables students to consolidate learning by applying theory to practice and identifying the skills, knowledge and personal traits which will help them succeed as a graduate practitioner. Chapters address a wealth of topical issues relating to both the development of the child and the student's own professional development. Areas of focus include ethical practice, safeguarding and child protection, the voice of the child, the role of the mentor, observation, assessment and the social and cultural factors which may impact on a child's development.

Including reflective activities, practical tips and examples of student experience throughout, this is an essential text for all early years students as they make the transition from academic study to professional practice.

Samantha McMahon is Principal Lecturer and Complex Pathway Leader for a range of early years courses at the University of Huddersfield, UK.

Mary Dyer is Senior Lecturer in Early Years at the University of Huddersfield, UK.

Advanced Work-based Practice in the Early Years

A Guide for Students

Edited by
Samantha McMahon and Mary Dyer

Routledge
Taylor & Francis Group

LONDON AND NEW YORK

First published 2019
by Routledge
2 Park Square, Milton Park, Abingdon, Oxon OX14 4RN

and by Routledge
711 Third Avenue, New York, NY 10017

Routledge is an imprint of the Taylor & Francis Group, an informa business

© 2019 selection and editorial matter, Samantha McMahon and Mary Dyer individual chapters, the contributors.

The right of Samantha McMahon and Mary Dyer to be identified as the authors of the editorial material, and of the authors for their individual chapters, has been asserted in accordance with sections 77 and 78 of the Copyright, Designs and Patents Act 1988.

All rights reserved. No part of this book may be reprinted or reproduced or utilised in any form or by any electronic, mechanical, or other means, now known or hereafter invented, including photocopying and recording, or in any information storage or retrieval system, without permission in writing from the publishers.

Trademark notice: Product or corporate names may be trademarks or registered trademarks, and are used only for identification and explanation without intent to infringe.

British Library Cataloguing-in-Publication Data
A catalogue record for this book is available from the British Library

Library of Congress Cataloging-in-Publication Data
Names: McMahon, Samantha, editor. | Dyer, Mary Kay, 1946– editor.
Title: Advanced work-based practice in the early years : a guide for students / edited by Samantha McMahon and Mary Dyer.
Description: Abingdon, Oxon : New York, NY : Routledge, 2019. | Includes bibliographical references and index.
Identifiers: LCCN 2018018798 (print) | LCCN 2018035693 (ebook) | ISBN 9780815396550 (hbk) | ISBN 9780815396567 (pbk) | ISBN 9781351181648 (ebk)
Subjects: LCSH: Early childhood teachers—Training of. | Early childhood education—Study and teaching (Higher)
Classification: LCC LB1775.6 (ebook) | LCC LB1775.6 .A37 2019 (print) | DDC 372.21—dc23
LC record available at https://lccn.loc.gov/2018018798

ISBN: 978-0-8153-9655-0 (hbk)
ISBN: 978-0-8153-9656-7 (pbk)
ISBN: 978-1-351-18164-8 (ebk)

Typeset in Sabon
by codeMantra
Printed by CPI Group (UK) Ltd, Croydon CR0 4YY

Contents

Acknowledgments

As editors of this book, we recognise that it is only through the efforts and contributions of others that it has been produced. We would therefore like to thank the chapter authors for sharing their expertise and finding the time to commit this to paper for the benefit of future early years practitioners. We would also like to thank the current early years practitioners, teachers and students who have generously offered their time and experiences so that policy, research and theory can be understood in terms of real world practice. Between you, you have enabled us to produce an engaging and informative book which will support the professional education of practitioners to come.

Samantha McMahon
Mary Dyer

Chapter 1

Ethical practice in the early years

Mary A. Dyer

CHAPTER AIMS

By the end of this chapter you will:

- understand how pedagogic strategies and care values contribute towards ethical and professional practice
- understand the relationship between ethical practice and personal values
- identify the personal values that underpin your own practice and understand how to reflect on and challenge them.

Introduction

It is easy to imagine that when early years students and practitioners are asked what they consider ethical practice to mean, that they focus on matters of policy, legislation and research protocols, identifying issues of confidentiality and anonymity in data gathering and information sharing, and the safe storage of data. They may also bring into their discussions the need to respect parents' wishes, and their own professional responsibilities for safeguarding and child protection. However, although these are key elements in ethical early years practice, they can sometimes give the misleading impression that ethical practice is a matter of process and policy, rather than one of personal values for individual practitioners. This can also lead students to believe that ethics and values are more usually concerned with issues of care and relationships rather than the supporting and assessment of learning.

This chapter considers how the practitioner's understanding of the child and childhood, and the purpose of early years provision inform practice. It explores how policy, pedagogy and personal values can be combined to develop an understanding of good practice through critical reflection, offering you a context within which to evaluate how you support young children's learning and holistic development, and how you decide what is important and ethical in your own practice. We begin by addressing the question of what is ethical practice in the early years, going on to consider the policy and pedagogical contexts for understanding ethical practice and end by considering how critical reflection can support you in articulating your own understanding of ethics in early years practice. In doing so, the chapter draws on literature that stresses the need for practitioners to apply and develop their own ethical stance not only to how they care for the children they work with and form relationships with, but also to their practice in supporting and assessing learning for these children.

What do we mean by 'ethical practice'?

Palaiologou (2012, p. 22) argues that ethical practice in the early years encompasses both how we practice, and how we conduct research 'through morally upright practices and how different points of view are considered'. This introduces the notion that the voice and interests of the child are significant when considering what ethical practice means. An example of this can be seen in this narrative from a Children's Centre practitioner:

> there was a practitioner, when it was snowing and there was obviously lots of ice on the floor and a 2½-year-old toddled outside and started playing in the ice and the snow … at which point the practitioner straightaway put the child in an all-in-one suit, wellingtons, took them outside, collected some snow and ice, came back in and continued that by getting ice out of the freezer that had got animals in it and extending that child's interest … that practitioner took the time and could see what that child actually wanted to do and was interested in and the whole time she was talking and explaining and really extended what he was enjoying doing … [closing the door] does keep the child warm but the child was also warm when she wrapped him up and took him outside. And that [closing the door] would just have, to me, would've been 'your interests aren't worth exploring and not valued.
>
> (Early Years Practitioner)

Palaiologou's definition also introduces a moral dimension to early years practice, a sense of personal value about right and wrong ways to practise, and about respect not just for the wishes and needs of parents/carers and colleagues, but also for those of young children. This may appear to introduce a tension between practice that meets the immediate needs of a child, and practice that supports their longer-term benefit, as shown in this narrative from a practitioner working in a school setting:

> you'll be timetabled to play with the role play with the children and to encourage them to use it properly … rather than run round playing drums with the cauldron which they might like to do, we have to kind of try and direct the play to the focus as it's intended … They're only allowed to wear their dressing up shoes for inside, they're not allowed to then go outside … I would love to let them do that … it's part of how they learn, how they develop and they could be engaged … sometimes it's so sad to make them take things off before they go outside because they might have dressed up in something inside and they're building their own role play in their home corner and then they want to take it outside and continue it and then you've got to stop them and say 'No take that off, that stays inside.
>
> (Classroom Support Worker)

For this practitioner, the right of children to lead their own play is overlooked by the need for adults to direct their learning. It is the responsibility of the practitioner to determine which of these needs are most pressing and how this balance may be achieved, based on their personal understanding of childhood and their own professional role.

Good practice, Palaiologou (2012) also reminds us, requires first an understanding of what we mean by good, in relation to how we perceive the child and their place in the social world. A perception of children as 'social actors, having agency, belonging to a unique culture and engaged in worthwhile, meaningful social relationships' (Palaiologou, 2012, p. 20), implies an acceptance that they are active participants in constructing *their* understanding of *their* world, individuals *with whom* rather than *on whom* we practice, which changes how we behave towards them. Neither of the two practitioners above has used the terms 'ethical practice' or 'values' in their narratives, but it is clear from the practice they describe what they approve of and what they are critical of. Their judgement is based on how the rights and interests of individual children are respected, and how this is reflected in the learning opportunities they are offered. Constructing children as capable and knowing individuals with shared responsibility for their learning shapes the experiences and interactions we offer them in early years settings, and influences the pedagogic strategies that underpin our practice.

ACTIVITY

Explain how you would support children aged 18–30 months in dressing.

- Which is quicker (and for the adult, easier) – letting a child work out how to put their socks on for themselves, or doing it for them?
- Does your approach envisage children as capable learners who can work things out for themselves or as unknowing individuals who need to be instructed and supervised?

Similarly, practitioners who understand the importance of emotionally stable and supportive environments often describe this in terms of what children need rather than as an ethical stance or personal value underpinning their own practice:

I think children should come to the setting and be happy all the time ... children come to us and they come from really disadvantaged backgrounds and unfortunately that smile [my smile] might be the only smile they see throughout that day so it's important that if they're only with us for 3 hours they have 3 hours of happiness.

(Day Nursery Deputy Manager)

if the children are coming into the setting and the staff aren't getting on then that's not good for the children ... if you haven't got a happy team you haven't got a happy setting ... and children will notice when things aren't good.

(Pre-school Manager)

For both these practitioners, meeting children's emotional needs is as important a part of good or ethical practice as meeting their cognitive needs, and cannot be overlooked. Relationships with young children, and the care and emotional support they receive are integral to an understanding of ethical practice. Taggart (2014) describes the role of the practitioner as being 'to water the seed of human flourishing itself and to foster compassion in future society', arguing strongly for an affective, emotional connection between practitioner and child.

What this means for practitioners is that they need to attend not only to the observation, planning and assessment required to support children's learning, but also that they need to consider how they respond to children as individuals and meet their care needs. Care and affection have been identified by many researchers as vital to young children's holistic development, from Bowlby's attachment theory that underpins key person working, to pedagogic issues (Ang, 2014; Taggart, 2014; Luff and Kanyal, 2015) that shape your interactions and engagement with children. The importance of practitioner-child relationships has been acknowledged not only in research (Page, 2011; Elfer and Page, 2013) but also in early years policy and legislation (DfE, 2017).

Policy context for ethical practice

Initial vocational training at NVQ Level 3 makes clear to would-be practitioners their responsibilities in terms of safeguarding and protecting children, data protection, and health and safety, as well as their role in providing a stimulating and supportive learning environment. Critical evaluation and a deeper understanding of these responsibilities, as well as the policies and legislation that support them, follow at degree level. The statutory EYFS framework (DfE, 2017) sets out the regulatory framework for all registered providers to adhere to, and Ofsted inspections are there to ensure these rules are followed. However, this legislative framework does not clearly address the issue raised above by Palaiologou (2012) of practitioners defining for themselves an ethical understanding of 'good', based on their own perceptions of the position of the child in our society and the kind of childhood they should experience.

The overarching principles of the EYFS

Three of the overarching principles of the early years foundation stage (EYFS) (DfE, 2017, p.6) offer a basis for understanding how practitioners might frame their understanding of children, and what ethical practice should encompass for the practitioner:

- The Unique Child
- Positive Relationships
- The Enabling Environment.

These three recognise children's individuality, the importance of relationships, and the role played by the physical and interpersonal or emotional environment of the setting in supporting children's healthy, holistic development. They bring together not only children's emotional and social needs but also their learning needs. They are an integral part of the statutory welfare requirements for early years practice

(DfE, 2017) but there is little specific guidance on how they are to be fulfilled. This is a matter of judgement for individual practitioners, based on their own values, cultural practices and perceptions of the child. We know that practitioners' failure to respect any one of these principles risks undermining and damaging children's developmental progress, and breaches professional practice standards and legislative requirements. Therefore, practitioners need to ensure that they understand how to underpin their practice with these principles. This can include taking time to get to know children, their interests, their families, their likes and dislikes; paying attention to which children play and socialise together; recognising and accommodating the individual learning needs and personalities of the children they work with; and understanding that an enabling environment is as much a matter of emotions and interactions as it is physical resources.

Key person approach

Key person working, a statutory requirement of the EYFS (DfE, 2017, p. 22) is recognised as an effective means of ensuring these three principles are embedded in practice:

The role of the key person

Each child must be assigned a key person. Their role is to help ensure that every child's care is tailored to meet their individual needs ... to help the child become familiar with the setting, offer a settled relationship for the child and build a relationship with their parents.

(DfE, 2017, pp. 22, 23)

The responsibility of the key person in settling a child into an early years setting cannot be underestimated, and it is based on a relationship between practitioner and child that takes time to develop. You need to consider how you can respond to a child as a unique individual, recognise their learning and development needs and their capabilities, and encourage in them a sense of belonging within the setting. Page (2011, p. 313) describes such a relationship as *'professional love'* (her italics), characterised as a relationship between practitioner and child that is 'deep, sustaining, respectful and reciprocal'. She goes on to argue that it complements the love a child receives from their parents and in matching what parents want or need for their children whilst attending the early years setting, represents ethical practice. Such a deep relationship requires effort and commitment on the part of the practitioner, an issue identified by Elfer and Page (2013) as causing anxiety for some. It is a very personal element of your practice, which may be undervalued by some as appearing to be based on instinct rather than knowledge and understanding (Manning-Morton, 2006), but which represents a vital element of your role.

Key person working is much more than a matter of staff deployment and workloads within a setting, and requires training, mentoring and support for practitioners if it is to be effective. However, by forming this relationship with specific children, and acknowledging the need of all children to be supported in this way, you are taking the first step in shaping your interactions and pedagogic approaches to practice from an ethical and values-based stance.

ACTIVITY

You are the key person for a 2-year-old child who is just starting to attend your setting for 3 days a week. This is the first setting this child has attended and the first time he/she will be separated from his/her mother.

- Make a list of what you might need to know about this child to help them settle, and how you would get this information.
- What might you do in order to help this child settle – either before they start attending regularly or as they arrive on their first day?
- Review your lists of information and activities – what do you think this indicates about your perception of young children and their needs? How does it reflect your own personal values?

Pedagogy and ethical practice

Just as a key person approach can provide some structure for an ethical stance to your practice, so too can the pedagogic approaches and strategies you adopt. Pedagogy can be defined as 'the understanding of how children learn and develop, and the practices through which we can enhance that process' (Stewart and Pugh, 2007, cited in DCSF, 2009, p. 4) or more simply as 'any activity that promoted learning' (Stephen, 2006, cited in Allen and Whalley, 2010, p. 13). Whilst these definitions might appear to suggest that pedagogy is concerned solely with the supporting of learning, the holistic needs of children and their position in their social and cultural world are also significant factors to be considered when making pedagogic decisions. The pedagogic approaches we use reflect what we know about children's developmental needs, and how we understand them as learners, as well as the role they actively play in their own learning. Some key questions for a practitioner to consider include:

- Are children individuals with no knowledge, and no capacity to acquire knowledge on their own?
- Are they active problem solvers, bringing past experience to new situations, and developing their own strategies for coping with new challenges, albeit with some support and help from those around them?
- What is the role of the practitioner –
  - to fill children with knowledge and skill?
  - to facilitate their learning of knowledge and skill in their own way?
  - to provide experiences that support them in understanding their social world?
  - to provide children with an educational programme that prepares them for entry to school?

You should not assume that you can only do one or the other in your practice, but your answers will determine the pedagogic strategies you use to underpin your practice, and reflect your perception of children's place in the social world.

Promoting social participation through ethical pedagogy

The pedagogic choices you make will not only support children in meeting the Early Learning Goals and developing a positive disposition towards their learning. Taggart (2014) argues that practitioners have an important role to play in reducing the vulnerability of the child and enabling them to participate more fully in their society. Whilst this is achieved in part through children gaining knowledge about their world, it also requires that you perceive the child as capable rather than incomplete, accepting that they can exercise agency in their learning rather than simply being subject to structural constraints (see Chapter 2 for further discussion of these concepts), and value their construction of their world. This requires an ethical approach to practice and pedagogy that 'attends to both the emotional quality of relationships and also to social justice'. By being genuinely respected and valued by those around them, Taggart (2014) argues, children will learn to respect and value others, and therefore be better equipped for social participation. Equally, by acknowledging the right of children to participate in society, they learn that they are worthwhile and valued.

THINKING ACTIVITY

Consider these two questions in relation to your own practice:

- How are you encouraging children to value each other and themselves in their interactions?
- What do you do in your practice that encourages children's wider social participation?

Now read through the behaviour policy in your setting, and reflect on the following points:

- How much of this policy is about managing the behaviour of 'rule breakers'?
- How much have the children themselves contributed to the development of this policy?
- What could you change in this policy to support practitioners to promote positive, ethical values in their practice?

The ethics of the educational relationship

Luff and Kanyal (2015, p. 11) argue that 'an affective model of early childhood pedagogy ... can have ethics of care at its ideological centre', achieved through attentive and reciprocal relationships between practitioner and child. Affect in psychological terms refers to emotional connections between individuals – liking, love and affection, and a close personal relationship. Noddings had earlier argued that care and an emotional connection with a learner should be understood as a form of relational ethics (Noddings, 1988, p. 218), and were essential for effective educational practice. She described effective teaching as a matter not of duty but of love – what today we might refer to as personal commitment to our learners and their progress, and positive regard for their well-being – noting that an approach to education based on respectful and affectionate interpersonal relationships takes time to develop. She identified a series of pedagogic strategies for such an approach which included 'modelling, dialogue, practice, and confirmation', all of which are familiar to early years practitioners. In many ways, it could be argued that what she identified was the key person approach and the pedagogic strategies used in early years practice today. Pedagogy, then, is not simply a matter of deciding how best to support children to achieve the Early Learning Goals (Early Education/DfE 2012), but requires values-led judgements about how our actions best fit our understanding of young children as learners in general, and their unique and individual needs in particular.

Other writers have also argued for the connection between care and an emotional connection with children, and the pedagogic approaches and strategies used in early years practice, to identify ethical approaches to practice. Ang (2014) gives a clear account of the research that supports the role of social and emotional development and well-being in underpinning children's learning, arguing that effective practice should be ethically situated in positive and supportive interpersonal relationships. She goes on to argue that the core of the practitioner role is to take account of the individuality of the child in their practice and their planning, echoing the principles of the EYFS (DfE, 2017). Luff and Kanyal (2015) further argue that this means practitioners have a duty to interpret the EYFS, and the statements set out in *Development Matters* (Early Education/DfE, 2012) to meet children's unique needs. This would mean that your planning of early years provision is personalised and differentiated for individual children, rather than assuming that practice appropriate for one child will meet the needs of all children.

ACTIVITY

- Review an activity plan you have recently used, and identify where you have personalised it to meet the needs and interests of individual children.
- Did you do enough to take account of different needs and interests – could you have done more?

Luff and Kanyal's (2015, p. 1) pedagogy of 'care-full values, that offers nurture for children and promotes peace, respect and concern for one another' echoes Noddings' (1988) integration of care and education as equal dimensions of the one pedagogic activity, and may be reflected in practice through the sensitivity of the practitioner to the emotional needs of an individual child, as seen in the narrative below:

There was one little boy who she'd got, I think he was just nearly 4, and he didn't speak, didn't speak anything, wouldn't speak to the other childminder, barely spoke to his mum and dad … I could see him edging towards me and then, he shied away … and I thought 'this little boy's trying to come to me, he wants to connect but he's scared of the other children … Maybe if I sit with him give him some one to one maybe he will start to open up a bit more … every morning for that next week I sat down with the puppet book, the same book because I could see him interested, … and he edged a bit further … and he got closer and closer, then by Friday he was sat next to me; … from what I'd seen of him it was the puppets and the voices that were making him interact … I found one with a teddy with the rhyme in Teddy Turns Round and Round, … and I did the rhyme with teddy bear and the little boy started holding the bear's hand … I said 'Do you want to have the bear?' and he kind of nodded, got the bear … and he was doing the rhyme with the bear.

(Childminder)

This childminder recognises that she needs to build a relationship with a child before he will trust her enough to engage with her and the other children, and that if she does not do this, he will not make progress in his learning and development. Her understanding of his developmental needs and her respectful and sensitive interactions with him are what make her practice effective, demonstrating that pedagogy is more effective when underpinned by care.

THINKING ACTIVITY

What do you think might have happened if:

- there was no space for him next to the practitioner?
- the practitioner had not realised he liked bears, puppets and rhymes and had chosen another book, for example, The Hungry Caterpillar?
- the practitioner had spoken directly to the little boy and asked him to sit next to her, or next to another child?

The ethics of co-construction and listening

Ethical practice is not just a matter of responding sensitively to the needs of individual children and reflecting this in the pedagogic strategies used to support their learning, or taking the time to build positive and affectionate relationships with them. It is also seen in the overall pedagogic approaches selected by practitioners, which reflect their perception of the place of children in society and their agency within their own learning. The key question to consider here is whether or not children are accorded the right to construct their own understanding of the world, or if this is decided for them by adults. Dahlberg and Moss (2005) argued that children should be regarded as agents within their own learning, and that the early years setting was a site for the co-construction of meaning, rather than a place where children were told how to understand the world. They proposed a 'pedagogy of listening' where practice was embedded in the relationship between practitioner and child, and where difference, choice and individuality were respected. Again, this pedagogic approach requires the interpretation of the EYFS and the changing of practice to meet the individual needs of children, rather than the expectation that activities which are appropriate for one child being appropriate for all. An example of this can be seen in in the following narrative from a pre-school manager, describing how long-standing practice was brought up to date by a group of children:

> We have a maypole ... usually a made up thing, it's a broom sticking up, and it works and we have it outside and we play some sort of folk type music. This year we have 2 or 3 very much boy, you know – boys ... they weren't interested in joining the maypole, they wanted to have air guitars at the side, so we thought 'well they are obviously not really interested and we need to follow their interests'. They thought it was namby pamby, these 3 boys, and they are worldly wise. So we set up a rock band and ... The X-Factor was talked about quite a bit so we decided we'd have a rock band and an X Factor show... I'm not saying we still didn't do the maypole dance with some of the children. But that afternoon we set up a rock band and we followed their lead and we got a real lot of information from them. They were making up names for themselves, they were counting to the beat, I feel it went completely off what we planned but we followed their lead and we made a whole display about it all ... off set of that we use instruments more, so it's being open as a practitioner to follow the children's lead and not be too tight on what you expect of them really.
>
> (Pre-school manager)

In acknowledging the interests of the children, and accepting that they had a right to direct their own learning, this represents an ethical choice made by the practitioner to follow the lead of the children. As a result, it has been possible to see children make progress with their learning whilst being fully engaged in play-based activities, as well as being valued as co-constructors of their own learning. Their sense of place in the world and their sense of agency and competence have all been supported alongside planned learning outcomes associated with rhythm, number and sound. This is particularly important for practitioners since the EYFS requires that children are assessed against the Characteristics of Effective Learning (CEL) (DfE, 2017, p. 10) as well as the Early Learning Goals, within a framework underpinned as much by principles of care as by areas of development and learning. As Noddings (1988) argued, educational practice is most effective when underpinned by positive relationships.

Turning personal values and ethics into professional practice standards

So far in this chapter, you have encountered a number of arguments about what ethical practice might mean for an early years practitioner, seen examples of how practitioners apply their own values to practice, and been encouraged to examine and challenge some of your own ideas and practice in relation to ethical values. The purpose of this chapter is not to tell you what your values should be, but to demonstrate that they can and will influence your practice. It is therefore important that as a practitioner you are aware of your own values and ethical stance, and take time to critically reflect on them and, where appropriate, challenge them. Since Manning-Morton (2006) tells us that the personal is professional for an early years practitioner, you need to spend time considering the relationship between the two and how it impacts on your practice.

Contextualising your reflections

Murray (2013) cautions that when practitioners rely solely on their personal values and ethics for the evaluation of their practice, they risk undermining the 'social legitimacy' of their work and their professional identity. She argues that practitioners should instead reflect on these values in the context of social, cultural and political expectations so that practice is developed in relation to a range of perceptions and expectations, including those of service users and regulators. This places a responsibility on you as a practitioner to be aware of the social and political context of your practice, to keep up to date with policy and regulatory developments, and to remain sensitive to the expectations of parents/carers, schools and other partner agencies and organisations. An ethical practitioner, then, is an informed practitioner. This way, even if the result of your reflection is to decide to develop your practice in contradiction of the expectations of others, this adds validity to any decisions you might make.

As well as a 'real world' context for your reflections, to achieve effective and usable evaluations of your relationships with children, you will need to contextualise them in terms of research and theory. Moss (2006) argued that practitioners' focus on the care element of their role led to them being perceived as acting on instinct rather than knowledge, and undermined the educational role they fulfilled. As this chapter has demonstrated, care is much more than a matter of instinct, and represents an ethical stance taken by practitioners to underpin the pedagogic choices they make when supporting children's learning. Critical reflection on your values, in relation to sociological, child development and pedagogic theory, can support you in developing a clear understanding of your own ethical stance in relation to your practice, and how this shapes your interactions with children. Ang (2014) advises that practitioners need to use reflection to 'unpick' and rationalise their affective connections with children. In other words, you need to consider your interactions with children in the context of research that identifies how the nature and quality of practitioner/child relationships contribute to their learning and development. To reflect simply in terms of your personal satisfaction or perception of the relationship will not provide sufficient scope for challenging your practice and developing it.

Reflective models for challenging your values

Critical reflection on practice requires first that you have some sense of what your practice should be, and that there is something about your practice that stands out (Dyer and Firth, 2018) – either for failing to live up to your expectations, or for proving to be especially effective in achieving your goals or meeting your standards. When reflecting on the ethical and personal values that underpin your practice, this process is more than one of simply evaluating your efficient use of time and resources, or whether or not you have met specific outcomes with regard to children's learning and developmental process. Critical refection on your values base and ethical stance requires you to delve much deeper into the motivations for your interactions, and your decision making, the reflection that Goodman (1984) would identify as Level 3, concerned with social justice, empowerment and emancipation. By reflecting at this level, you are seeking a more personal level of justification for what you consider to be acceptable practice, which although located in a social and policy context, is your own statement of belief or value.

Whilst the processes and approaches used for reflection are very much a matter of personal choice (Dyer and Firth, 2018), there are some models that offer a supportive structure for you to follow in attempting to reflect in such depth. Brookfield's Lenses (Brookfield, 2002) requires that you systematically critique your practice from a range of perspectives, including your own, those of the people you work with (this would include any child/children as one perspective, and colleagues and/ or families as a separate perspective) and that of appropriate theory and research. By doing so, you are encouraged to consider the impact of your interactions on others, and the expectations they may have of you and your practice. This then can challenge you to justify the appropriateness of your actions, and to understand how others perceive your role.

The apparently straightforward model (Rolfe et al., 2001) of 'What, so what, now what' similarly provokes you to consider the impact of your actions and interactions on others, by focusing on the consequences of your actions. You can use this model to describe your actions (what), explain your motivation and intentions as well as the outcomes (so what) and consider the effectiveness of this and/or how your practice will change in future (now what). By using a theoretical context at all three stages in this model to explain and justify your interactions, you should find yourself able to give a theory-based rationale for your practice, moving it from instinct and personal disposition to the application of a critical understanding of research and theory.

Finally, Johns' model for structured reflection (Johns, 2004) presents you with a series of questions to answer which result in an in-depth consideration of the many different possible underpinning motivations for your actions. His model poses such questions as:

- How were others feeling, and what made them feel that way?
- What was I trying to achieve and did I respond effectively?
- What knowledge did or might have informed me?
- To what extent did I act for the best and in tune with my values?

(Johns, 2004, p. 18)

Although this model was developed for use in the nursing profession, its focus on personal interactions and the values that underpin them makes it especially useful for early years practitioners working with young children who may not always be able to express their needs easily, and whose wishes therefore may at times get overlooked. Again, the model directs you not only to consider your own intentions and motivations, but also a theoretical or knowledge based context for your actions.

Whichever approach you chose to follow for your reflections, the essential elements are:

- a range of different perspectives on your actions – even if this means approaching individuals and asking them to tell you this themselves
- a theoretical context for explaining your actions and interactions, your values, your intentions
- a theoretical context for justifying your conclusions about your practice
- a theoretical context for justifying future action or change to practice.

Whilst this makes critical reflection a lengthier process, it will also make it a more meaningful and useful process to you. Not only will it increase your awareness of the values that underpin your practice, but it will also empower you to justify the ethical stance you take in your practice, as you interpret the EYFS to meet children's individual learning needs.

Conclusion

Ethical practice in early years provision then, is more than simply a matter of maintaining confidentiality and demonstrating respect for those we work with and for. It is a combination of personal values and a deep understanding of pedagogical theory that is put into practice when working with young children, as well as ensuring that appropriate legislation and policy is followed. The development of ethical practice is supported by careful and thoughtful reflection on your personal values, and your understanding of early years practice, sometimes challenging these, sometimes justifying them. Your undergraduate studies and your work experience can help you understand how these influence your practice, but only you can decide what these values should be. Take the time, as you complete your degree, to identify incidents that catch your attention and challenge your practice, and consider if what is being challenged is your knowledge of children and their learning and development, or your own perceptions and values about the work that you do. Such a reflection may not always be a comfortable one, but it is one which will make you a more ethical and empowered practitioner.

Additional reading

Palaiologou, I. (2012) *Ethical practice in early childhood*. London: Sage.

Taggart, G. (2014) Compassionate pedagogy: the ethics of care in early childhoodprofessionalism. *European Early Childhood Education Research Journal*, DOI: 10.1080/1350293X. 2014.970847

References

Allen, S. and Whalley, M. E. (2010) *Supporting pedagogy and practice in the early years*. Exeter: Learning Matters.

Ang, L. (2014) Pre-school or prep school? Rethinking the role of early years education. *Contemporary Issues on Early Childhood*, 15 (2), 185–199.

Brookfield, S. D. (2002) Using the lenses of critically reflective teaching in the community college classroom. *New Directions for Community Colleges*, 118, 31–38.

Dahlberg, G. and Moss, P. (2005) *Ethics and politics in early childhood education*. London: Routledge-Falmer.

Department for Education (DfE) (2017) *Statutory framework for the early years foundation stage: setting the standards for learning, development and care for children from birth to five*. London: Crown Copyright.

Dyer, M. and Firth, N. (2018) Being a reflective practitioner. In McMahon, S. and Dyer, M., *Work-based practice in the early years: a guide for students*. Abingdon: Routledge.

Early Education/DfE (2012) *Development matters in the early years foundation stage*. London: Crown Copyright.

Elfer, P. and Page, J. (2013) The emotional complexity of attachment interactions in nursery. *European Early Childhood Education Research Journal*, 21 (4), 553–567.

Goodman, J. (1984) Reflection and teacher education: a case study and theoretical analysis. *Interchanges*, 15, 9–26.

Johns, C. (2004) *Becoming a reflective practitioner*. 2nd edition. Oxford: Blackwell Publishing.

Luff, P. and Kanyal, M. (2015) Maternal thinking and beyond: towards a care-full pedagogy for early childhood. *Early Child Development and Care*, DOI: 10.1080/03004430.2015.1028389.

Manning-Morton, J. (2006) The personal is professional: professionalism and the birth to threes practitioner. *Contemporary Issues on Early Childhood*, 7 (1), 42–52.

Moss, P. (2006) Structure, understandings and discourses: possibilities for re-envisioning the early childhood worker. *Contemporary Issues on Early Childhood*, 7 (1), 30–41.

Murray, J. (2013) Becoming an early years professional: developing a new professional identity. *European Early Childhood Education Research Journal*, 21 (4), 527–540.

Noddings, N. (1988) An ethic of caring and its implications for instructional arrangements. *American Journal of Education*, 96 (2), 215–230.

Page, J. (2011) Do mothers want professional carers to love their babies? *Journal of Early Childhood Research*, 9 (3), 310–323.

Palaiologou I. (2012) *Ethical practice in early childhood*. London: Sage.

Rolfe, G., Freshwater, D. and Jaspar, M. (2001) *Critical reflection for nursing and helping professions*. Basingstoke: Palgrave.

Stephen, C. (2006) *Early Years Education: perspectives from a review of international literature*. Available from the Scottish Executive at www.scotland.gov.uk/Resource/Doc/92395/0022116.pdf (accessed 9 March 2018).

Stewart, N. and Pugh, R (2007) Early Years vision in focus, Part 2: exploring pedagogy. Copyright: Shropshire County Council. In Department for Children, Schools and Families (DCSF) (2009) *Learning, playing and interacting: good practice in the early years foundation stage*. London: Crown Copyright.

Taggart, G. (2014) Compassionate pedagogy: the ethics of care in early childhood professionalism. *European Early Childhood Education Research Journal*, DOI: 10.1080/1350293X.2014.970847.

Chapter 2

Social, cultural and economic factors shaping children's learning and development

Nicola Firth

CHAPTER AIMS

By the end of this chapter you will be able to:

- identify factors that influence children's learning and development
- analyse how children's learning and development can be affected when growing up in poverty and areas of deprivation
- examine how primary and secondary socialisation influences children's social, cultural and economic capital.

Introduction

All children are affected by social, cultural and economic factors that shape their learning and development. Some children will have positive experiences of these factors, but unfortunately in reality many children will be affected negatively. Children can be easily affected by these factors, as they are vulnerable and cannot take individual control of their daily lives and experiences at this young age. Decisions are made on behalf of children by adults, particularly their parents/carers, decisions which are shaped by structural and agency factors within society. Agency is about decisions and choices people make individually or sometimes as a family; and structure includes policies, legislation and services within society, controlled by more powerful bodies such as local authorities and government. An example of agency is if a person chooses not to work, so is therefore reliant on benefits. The structural factors here include welfare provision and the laws which the government will have passed to determine how much a person or family can claim whilst on benefits.

It is crucial that those working with children and their families within the care and education sector are aware of family circumstances. They should attempt to determine factors associated with structure and agency in terms of not only how the family can take control of their own lives (agency) but also how wider society and services can support them in enhancing their lives (structure). Early years educators and teachers are then better positioned to provide support and guidance in order for families to enhance social and cultural experiences and economic capital. This chapter will explore how children's learning and development can be impacted when there are issues relating to social, cultural and economic capital including poverty, care and education and family.

Social construct of childhood

It is important to briefly touch upon how childhood is constructed when considering factors that affect children's learning and development. Childhood has changed and developed over time, as Ariès (1962) suggested, 'childhood was not a natural or universal phenomenon, but one that varied according to time and place' (cited by Gabriel, 2017, p. 15). Every child has a different childhood, no two are the same and you must continually consider and reflect on this in your practice.

Childhood experiences across societies and countries differ, but sociologists tend to agree that children should be active in constructing their own lives, and on a social level this includes relationships with parents, family and friends (Gabriel, 2017). The United Nations Convention on the Rights of the Child (UNCRC) supports the concept of children constructing their own lives and having their own rights, views and opinions, relating directly to agency. Nonetheless this remains a hotly debated topic, since adults still make decisions for children, on their behalf, as children are still perceived as being unable to make informed decisions (Gabriel, 2017). Therefore, whilst in placement you need to be mindful of the influences on children's choices and just how much influence children have on social, cultural and economic factors that may be affecting them; not only parents/carers but the whole of society influence these factors, including early years educators and teachers working directly with children.

THINKING ACTIVITY

List the types of experiences and decisions that you or early years educators/ teachers have made for children attending your setting, for example meals and snacks, play equipment …

Now look back over the list and ask yourself, 'could children have been more involved in decision making for each experience'?

If children are unable to be part of decision making about their own lives, inequality becomes an issue. This can lead to discrimination in their everyday lives and they may receive unfair treatment by the others in society. Discrimination affects all areas of a child's development, as they may be excluded by others not only within their learning environment but also within their community and wider society. Throughout this chapter, inequality will be considered as a crucial factor in how individuals and groups are portrayed in and by society.

Poverty and deprivation

Poverty affects 1 in 4 children in the United Kingdom, which equates to 9 children in a classroom of 30 (Child Poverty Action Group [CPAG], 2017). Growing up in poverty affects both the short and long-term well-being of a child due to poor housing, health problems, limited participation in society and underachieving in education. Additional funding in schools and early years settings is available to disadvantaged children to raise educational attainment called Pupil Premium (GOV.UK, 2017). The following case study from a head teacher demonstrates how Pupil Premium can support children and some of the challenges working in a primary school in an area of poverty and deprivation can bring:

Case study

A head teacher's perspective of the challenges when working in a primary school in an area of deprivation.

Kate is a head teacher with 21 years' experience of teaching in primary schools. Kate worked initially as a teacher and was promoted to head teacher in the second school where she was employed. In total, Kate has worked in four primary schools, all based in areas of deprivation. All these schools have at some point been graded either 'requires improvement' or 'inadequate' by the Office for Standards in Education, Children's Services and Skills (Ofsted) whilst Kate has worked in them. However, Kate is optimistic after Ofsted have altered their focus on achievement, and inspectors will be monitoring Pupil Premium students as an isolated group, who will be measured on the progress they make from the level they start at in education, rather than expected outcomes.

From Kate's experience, challenges and factors affecting children's learning and development are related to:

- poverty
- poor housing
- lack of educational opportunities for parents
- barriers to education, as parents' experiences of school have not been positive so they transfer that on to their children or on to their relationship with the school
- poor parental support for their children
- chaotic households, for example domestic abuse, violence and substance misuse.

Kate has worked with a high number of children born into chaotic households, however this does not mean they will not engage in their education. Sometimes, children from chaotic households respond well to structure at school and benefit from clear boundaries. Nevertheless, many children who are in receipt of Pupil Premium have persistent absenteeism, and this has an enormous impact on their education as they are not in school to be educated.

A common delay in children's learning and development is language development, when coming from an area of deprivation. Kate regularly sees that children do not have key vocabulary in comparison to those growing up in more affluent areas where they might be read a bedtime story and parents have higher

(Continued)

expectations. This is particularly evident in the younger years when children are starting to attend school. Kate believes this has a persistent effect throughout the early years foundation stage and moves with them into the National Curriculum.

Emotional development can be a problem for the children and from Kate's experience this can be because their parents may have mental health issues due to where they live and their lifestyle. Kate has also found that the child may not have the same levels of nurture in comparison to a child coming from a household where parents have a better level of education and more money.

Support is available in all schools and early help can support children who require intervention through Pupil Premium. Kate believes Pupil Premium is really important and can be used from helping families buy uniforms to accessing support and intervention. This has increased children's access to not only educational activities but also their social and cultural capital, as they can be included more now in comparison to the past, as Pupil Premium can be used to support children going on school trips and accessing school enhancement activities. However, Kate feels frustrated that teachers do as much as they can in school, so children get the same entitlements, but in the home environment they cannot always intervene if the family do not want them to. Nonetheless, teachers can signpost to intervention and services, although not all families will engage with agencies and services and this is a huge barrier. In Kate's experience of early intervention, families often view early help as social workers 'knocking on their doors' and this is why they do not engage, as they find it threatening due to their own past experiences or because of things that might be happening in their lives at the current time such as substance misuse. Kate has, however, known many families that have engaged in early help and their lives have been transformed for the better.

Throughout the case study Kate relates to various examples of the social, cultural and economic factors that influence children's learning and development. It is imperative that in practice you are aware of these issues and how they impact on children's development, as they tend to have a negative influence. However, if families engage in support that can be provided or signposted to by early years care and education settings, this can have a positive influence, and as Kate says their lives can be 'transformed for the better'. This is where a family's agency can result in engaging with support services therefore they are supported by the structure of society. Legislation reinforces ways in which the government plan to tackle issues such as child poverty structurally.

Child poverty legislation

The Child Poverty Act 2010 aimed to eradicate child poverty by 2020, a Labour Government commitment made in September 2008. This was welcomed by all political parties. However, the Conservative Party, as part of the 2010 Coalition Government, argued the focus should be on underlying causes of child poverty (Kennedy, 2014). The Act was amended in 2012 in order to establish a Social Mobility and Child

Poverty Commission (CPAG, 2018), but in 2013 the Commission determined the target to eradicate child poverty by 2020 was going to be missed by a significant margin (Kennedy, 2014). The Conservative Government abolished the Child Poverty Act 2010 and replaced it with the Welfare Reform and Work Act 2016, which aims to reduce poverty based on the measurement of family income (CPAG, 2018). The Act has four main targets that are legally imposed on governments to act by 2020, including:

- relative poverty: no more that 10% of children living in relative low income families (net income lower than 60% of the UK median)
- absolute poverty: no more than 5% of children living in absolute low income
- combined low income and maternal deprivation: no more than 5% of children living in maternal deprivation and low income families (net income lower than 70% of the UK median)
- persistent poverty: fewer children living in relative poverty for a period of three years or more.

(CPAG, 2018)

THINKING ACTIVITY

Consider the aim of the Child Poverty Act 2010 to eradicate child poverty by 2020, and ask yourself the questions:

- Can child poverty ever be eradicated in a society where children's lives are controlled by adults making decisions for them?
- Was this aim ever achievable and can ending child poverty ever be achievable?

Absolute and relative poverty

Poverty is normally referred to as absolute or relative poverty, both of which are targeted in the Welfare Reform and Work Act 2016. Absolute poverty is measured by the amount of money available to meet minimum needs such as food, shelter and clothing whereas relative poverty relates to economic status in society and if a person or family is falling below 'prevailing standards of living' in a societal context (UNESCO, 2017). An example of this may be a family who do not earn enough to maintain an average standard of living in the society which they live. The family may not be able to afford family outings such as holidays, going to the cinema or buying essentials including new school uniforms and shoes. It is important to remember that relative poverty is measured against societal expectations so can differ between countries and over time. In England relative poverty outweighs absolute poverty and an example of those living in absolute poverty would be someone who is homeless.

The impact of both forms of poverty can be seen in Maslow's Hierarchy of Needs, where Maslow (1943) argues that a person's basic needs must be met in order for them to achieve the best out of life. The most basic needs are physiological, for example shelter, hunger and thirst, moving through to self-actualisation where Maslow considers a person's needs have been met and they will be satisfied with their life (Maslow, 1943).

Figure 2.1 Example of Maslow's Hierarchy of Needs (1943).

For a family living in absolute poverty, they would not meet the most basic standard of physiological needs. Although a family living in relative poverty would be able to meet the physiological needs, they will struggle on a day-to-day basis to be able to afford an average standard of living in order to meet the higher order needs which are safety needs, emotional needs, esteem needs and self-actualisation. Considering the hierarchy of needs, this type of family may find it difficult to reach even the second stage, safety needs, as they may not feel safe, for instance they may live in an area where crime is high therefore never achieving emotional needs, esteem needs and self-actualisation (Maslow, 1943). Maslow's Hierarchy of Needs has been criticised as considering only individual needs and not that of a person's social interactions and culture (Trigg, 2004). Over the years the hierarchy has been adapted by others such as Dukes and Smith (2009), who included an aesthetic needs and wants stage. The hierarchy, however, continues to be a theory that is related to in many disciplines relating to a person's needs.

THINKING ACTIVITY

Take some time to reflect on your own childhood and/or that of others you know. Were you and your family or friends affected by poverty? How did this impact on daily life and learning and development?

Write a list of how a child's learning and development can be affected by poverty. Can you link some of these to Maslow's Hierarchy of Needs and which stage the child may reach?

You can use the Hierarchy of Needs to assist in assessing where a child may be placed in terms of their needs. This will help you to understand what additional needs the child may have and be in a stronger position to signpost the family to appropriate support services and agencies, including access to Pupil Premium and other additional funding that may be available.

The next section of the chapter will explore how children's education can be affected by living in relative poverty, and other factors that impact on learning and development, including the quality of care and education settings, and the gender of the child.

Education and care

At age 16 when most young people are achieving GCSE's, those from poorer backgrounds are one third less likely to achieve good grades than their counterparts from more affluent families (Joseph Rowntree Foundation [JRF] 2017). This leads to a minority group of young people at a disadvantage in the labour market, as now more than ever there is an increase in people achieving higher education degrees: an increase of over 38% since 1996 in England (JRF, 2017). This is leaving those with fewer or no qualifications behind and they find it much harder to find a job, with many of them living on poor wages or reliant on benefits. Nevertheless, research evidences that the earlier a child has access to high quality care and education, educational outcomes can be significantly improved (Sylva et al., 2004; Taggart et al., 2015). Therefore with support that is now available for deprived children in their early years it is anticipated that GCSE performance will improve, resulting in better outcomes for young adults. You need to be mindful in your practice of this minority group and consider strategies that will support children and their families to feel empowered to improve their social, cultural and economic capital.

Pupil Premium and Early Years Pupil Premium

In 2011 the Coalition Government introduced the Pupil Premium aimed at school-aged disadvantaged children in order to raise attainment levels and close the gap between them and their peers, who have better standards of living (GOV.UK, 2017). Early Years Pupil Premium (EYPP) was then rolled out in 2015, available for 3- and 4-year-old children who meet benefit related criteria for free school meals, children looked after by the local authority and adopted children (Foster and Long, 2017). As alluded to in Kate's case study Pupil Premium and EYPP can be spent in various ways from supporting a family to purchase a school uniform and participating in enhancement activities to buying in external support services and agencies who can offer specialist advice and support to the child and their family. The Department for Education's Dedicated Schools Grant allocated £31 million in 2017/18 to local authorities to distribute to early years providers, to be spent to support disadvantaged children (Foster and Long, 2017), although this was a reduction from the £50 million made available in 2015/16, when first rolled out (GOV.UK, 2015). Ofsted have responsibility to report if early years providers have spent the funding effectively and this will be judged during inspections (GOV.UK, 2015). If and when families no longer meet Pupil Premium criteria children will still receive free school meals for another 6 years known as 'Ever 6 FSM' (GOV.UK, 2017). This is because the government have recognised it will take them time to move out of the poverty trap they may have found themselves in. It is important that early years providers encourage parents to complete information required to claim the funding, to ensure that all eligible children receive the funding, so they receive the additional support required. From this, it is expected that disadvantaged children will achieve better in their learning and enhance their social, cultural and economic capital as they grow up and move into post-compulsory education and chosen career paths.

Quality childcare and education

The Effective Provision of Pre-School Education (EPPE) reported back in 2004 that the earlier children access high quality childcare, the more educational outcomes are significantly improved (Sylva et al, 2004). The EPPE project concluded that when children aged 7 took their Statutory Attainment Tests (SATS), children who had received high quality childcare and education at a younger age not only achieved better educational attainment, but also had better social development and skills (Sylva et al 2004). This landmark research resulted in all 3- and 4-year-old children having access to a part-time place in pre-school since the start of this century. Unfortunately though, for some groups of children high quality childcare and education is not always available. The Centre for Analysis of Social Exclusion (CASE) found that although children from disadvantaged areas had access to more highly qualified early years practitioners and teachers, services that cater for disadvantaged children tend to be segregated and achieve lower ratings by Ofsted (Gambaro, Stewart and Waldfogel, 2013). There are more maintained nursery schools in inner city areas, where many disadvantaged children live but although this type of setting will have more highly qualified staff it will be measured by Ofsted on children's outcomes (Gambaro, Stewart and Waldfogel, 2013). Disadvantaged children's outcomes are frequently lower than those of children from families earning higher incomes (Mukherji and Dryden, 2014) therefore ratings by Ofsted influenced by this factor will result in the setting achieving a lower grade than one in a more affluent area. However, as Kate explains in the case study, Ofsted are changing the way inspections take place and will be focusing on children in receipt of Pupil Premium as an isolated group with their achievement being measured on progress rather than expected outcomes. With this revised inspection method Kate anticipates schools in areas of deprivation will be inspected more objectively in line with schools in more affluent areas and achieve better Ofsted grades.

Funded places for pre-school children

All 3- and 4-year-olds in England are entitled to free education and childcare equating to 15 hours per week for 38 weeks of the year. Some 3- and 4-year-olds are entitled to additional funding equating to 30 hours per week, however this is dependent on parents being in work for more than 16 hours per week and earning at least the minimum wage (GOV.UK, 2018b). This means some children who are underachieving in education will not be able to access these additional hours, if their parents are not in employment, resulting in unequal access to early education. However, CPAG (2018) report that 'two thirds of children growing up in poverty live in a family where at least one person works', therefore some disadvantaged children will be able to access additional hours in childcare and education, resulting in what may be better outcomes throughout education and in later life.

The Coalition Government introduced funding for some 2-year-olds in 2014. Eligibility criteria for this funding are dependent on welfare parents receive, for example, income support, job seekers allowance or universal credit. It is also available for looked after children and children who have an education, health and care plan (GOV.UK, 2018a). Looked after children and children with special educational needs (SEN) are also at disadvantage in terms of good educational achievement because of their additional needs and sometimes chaotic backgrounds, which can affect their social and emotional development at a very young age. The original aim from the Coalition Government for 2-year-old funding was to equip children with essential skills in order to be successful in later life (DfE, 2013). The funding though for 2-, 3- and 4-year-olds has caused problems, the main one being that nurseries actually lose money, as the funding available does not cover the cost of a place when compared to being paid for privately by parents. Gaunt (2015) reported 'chronic under-funding' with nurseries losing on average £800 per year per funded child. This has continued to be an issue and some nurseries charge additional costs, which may be unaffordable for a family living on benefits or minimum wage so that their child then may not be able to access early education, resulting in the possibility of poorer educational outcomes (Sylva et al., 2004; Taggart et al., 2015). This is also a form of discrimination and the needs of young children not being met by the structure of the wider society.

Gender issues in early education

For some time girls have been outperforming boys educational achievement; boy's underachievement hit media headlines after league tables for primary education in England were published back in 1996 (Mills et al., 2009). This issue has continued to dominate current educational policy and it was not until some 17 years later that statistical data was published for children in the early years foundation stage, and again it was recognised boys were underperforming in comparison to girls across all areas of learning in their early years (DfE, 2014). Upon analysis of statistical data released for 2013/14 by the DfE (2014), girls outperformed boys by 17% within the early years foundation stage profile, with 69% of girls achieving a good level of development in comparison to 52% of boys. This was the first data set that had been made available after the introduction of the revised early years foundation stage in 2012. Data for 2014/2015 showed a slight reduction in the gender gap; both boys and girls had increased in achievement but boys at a slightly faster rate (DfE, 2015). Evidence of this trend continued into 2015/2016 with 59.7% of boys achieving their expected level in the early learning goals in comparison to 75.4% of girls achieving (DfE, 2016). It remains to be a concern, though, that boys continue to perform less well than girls in all areas of learning, and this is impacting on their learning and development.

Pascal and Bertram (2016b) led a research project on how young white working class boys' educational achievement may be enhanced, as it was recognised this group are more likely to be underachieving. Their project followed forty boys whose families were living on low incomes but the boys were achieving well in education. The aim was to 'generate new knowledge about behaviours and interactions for learning enhancement in homes and early education settings' (Pascal and Bertram, 2016b, p. 4). This research is different to many others, as the researchers focused on achieving boys rather than underachieving boys. The research team observed interactions within the home environment and relationships between the parent and child. Some of the boys came from quite chaotic homes, but findings indicated that as long as the boys had at least one core relationship within the home they had high resilience, supporting educational achievement. Also key to the findings were that most of the boys had attended 2-year-old funded places and developed strong bonds with key persons. The parents of the boys talked about how they had been supported as a family by high quality provision led by practitioners (Pascal and Bertram, 2016a), very similar to the findings of the EPPE project (Sylva et al., 2004). These findings suggest that if support is provided in the home environment by at least one core relationship and a high quality early education setting, boys have the potential to achieve and even with issues relating to social, cultural and economic capital learning and development can be enhanced.

In practice you need to be aware of the gender achievement gap when planning for children's learning, and consider how boys and girls may learn and develop in different ways. Observing children's interests and planning activities that engage both genders is fundamental to effective planning and to enhancing their learning, and development. If children become disengaged in education in the very early years, this may continue through the whole of their education and reduce access to social, cultural and economic capital.

Family and the community

A child's family is crucial in providing for and influencing their childhood, learning and development, through **primary socialisation**, provided by immediate family, and friends closest to the child. This is where the child will learn about values and beliefs and is influenced by culture and background. **Secondary socialisation** is the wider relationships a child will develop with others such as nursery, school and the community they live in. Both types of socialisation are important factors in how the child develops throughout their early years, and learning and development can be enhanced or reduced by experiences from any party. This is further explained by Bronfenbrenner's Ecological Systems Theory, which considers how the environment can affect children's learning and development (Mukherji and Dryden, 2014). The child sits within four systems and is seen as an active agent influenced by the different systems:

- Microsystem – relationships associated closest to the child, including family, friends and early education settings
- Mesosystem – this interconnects with the microsystem and includes the local community, considering support mechanisms that can directly relate to the child and their family
- Exosystem – relates to those the child may not have any direct contact with but still influences the child's development, such as local government making decisions about services related to the child, i.e. local early childhood and education services or health services
- Macrosystem – related to much wider society and decisions made at a national or global level, for example laws and policies.

(Mukherji and Dryden, 2014)

Primary socialisation influences are located in the micro-system, most directly connected to the child, and as the systems move further away from the child, influences are connected to secondary socialisation. Being aware of these influences can support you in assessing a child's social, cultural and economic capital, placing you in a stronger position to develop relationships with children and their families, and meeting children's learning and developmental needs.

THINKING ACTIVITY

Draw your own diagram of the Ecological Systems Theory. In each system write individuals, groups and organisations that can affect a child's social, cultural and economic capital. Think of ways in which they may impact on a child's learning and development and if these represent structure or agency.

Family

Family structures have changed and are much more diverse compared to that of the nuclear family, which was the most common type of family only 40 years ago (Gabriel, 2017). The nuclear family consisted of father, mother and children living in the same household. However this is no longer the dominant family type and other family types have formed including single-parent families, reconstituted families and same-sex couple families. The family has evolved, and it is much more common for both men and women to be employed, rather than the male working and being the breadwinner, as in the past. This has changed how young children are brought up, with many more children attending early care and education settings. A shift has taken place within the social, cultural and economic factors that affect and shape the family unit.

All family types are unique and form a child's primary socialisation. Nevertheless some are affected more than others when considering social, cultural and economic capital. Single-parent families and families with three or more children are more likely to be affected by poverty (JRF, 2017). Reasons why include:

- only one income coming into the household for a single-parent family
- the costs associated with having three or more children in comparison to only having one or two children
- single-parent and large families are more likely to live in an area of deprivation.

A study conducted by the National Children's Bureau [NCB] found that children living in areas of deprivation have a higher rate of tooth decay, suffer from obesity, have a higher risk of injury and are less likely to be at a good level of development (GLD) before starting school (NCB, 2015). It is also reported by JRF (2017) that children living in lower income families do not always discuss important issues and are more likely to quarrel with their parents, and this will affect their emotional well-being. These factors not only relate to the family, but also the community: secondary socialisation influences. NCB (2015, p. 25) conclude that 'public health should be everyone's business' and recommend 'the development of effective local integrated systems and approaches are key for improving outcomes for children aged five and under'.

Local support for families

Key support services need to be available in areas of deprivation in order to intervene and educate families about their health and well-being. Unfortunately though, key services for children known as Sure Start Children's Centres (SSCC) have faced huge budget cuts resulting in closures. Bate and Foster (2017) in a Briefing Paper to Parliament reported that 208 SSCC had closed since 2015, however Blackman-Woods, a Labour MP, argued that since 2010 when the Coalition then Conservative Government came into power more than 800 SSCC had closed. The closure of SSCC continues to be a trend, resulting in a reduction of early years support for children and their families in local communities. This is a concerning factor when considering that currently poverty is affecting 1 in 4 children in the United Kingdom (CPAG, 2017). If less support is available for children and their families then the efforts to improve educational attainment for children living in poverty in areas of deprivation could face the risk of failure at a structural level. Considering this you must intervene early to provide support and meet children's learning and development needs.

Conclusion

Throughout this chapter the key topics explored have been poverty, care and education and family. These are all crucial factors which influence children's access to social, cultural and economic capital, which you need to be conscious of when on placement, and working in the early years care and education sector. Poverty is a key theme running throughout and it is important to consider how families struggling to afford even the basics in life are supported. The child is key within this context, as early influences shape their whole lives and it is recognised that early support and intervention can help. As Bronfenbrenner's theory considers how a child's environment influences their development, they should still be seen as an active agent within their own lives (Mukherji and Dryden, 2014) and it is your role to support the child. Therefore, you must understand structural policy such as 2-, 3- and 4-year-old funding and EYPP and how families can access additional funding, as they may not be aware. The support you provide can make a difference to the family's agency and recognition of structural support that can be provided.

It is apparent even in the 21st century inequality remains a key concern and various groups of people are affected by inequalities on a daily basis. Some of these groups have been considered in this chapter with a main focus on children living in areas of deprivation. Nevertheless, you must not forget other groups such as boys underachieving in education, children who have special educational needs and looked after children. It is not only those living in areas of deprivation that suffer from reduced access to social, cultural and economic capital and in placement you will also identify other groups that are affected in their learning and development by such factors. You must take time to find out about services and agencies in the local area in order to offer support, advice and guidance to children and families most vulnerable to reduced social, cultural and economic capital. With early support in place children's learning and development can be enhanced, increasing their chances of a better education, leading to higher qualifications and a good career. The family have agency to make decisions that will improve their lives and through the support of wider structural services the family may increase their social, cultural and economic capital.

Additional reading

Pascal, C. and Bertram, T. (2016) *High Achieving White Working Class (HAWWC) Boys Project: Final Report March 2016*. Birmingham: Centre for Research in Early Childhood. Findings of the project attempting to address the question of how educational achievement might be enhanced for young white working class boys in order to close the gap in their educational attainment.

Child Poverty Action Group: a charity working to understand what causes poverty, the impact it has on children's lives and how it can be solved. You will find up-to-date statistics and publications to support your learning. Their homepage page can be found at: www.cpag.org.uk/.

National Children's Bureau (2015) *Poor beginnings: health inequalities among young children across England*. London: National Children's Bureau. A report that challenges how and why growing up in certain parts of England a child under 5 is more likely to have poor health that will impact the rest of their lives.

References

Ariès, P. (1962) *Centuries of childhood*. London: Jonathan Cape.

Bate, A. and Foster, D. (2017) *Sure Start (England): Briefing Paper Number 7257, 9 June 2017*. London: House of Commons Library.

Child Poverty Action Group (CPAG) (2017) *Chid poverty facts and figures*. Available at: www.cpag.org.uk/child-poverty-facts-and-figures (date accessed: 6 January 2018).

Child Poverty Action Group (CPAG) (2018) *Child poverty promise and Child Poverty Act*. Available at: www.cpag.org.uk/content/child-poverty-promise-and-child-poverty-act (date accessed: 12 January 2018).

DfE (2013) *Press release: £755 million to double free childcare offer for 2-year-olds*. Available at: www.gov.uk/government/news/755-million-to-double-free-childcare-offer-for-2-year-olds (date accessed: 17 January 2018).

DfE (2014) Statistical first release: early years foundation stage profile results in England, 2013/14, London: DfE.

DfE (2015) Early years foundation stage profile results in England, 2015, London: DfE.

DfE (2016) Early years foundation stage profile results in England, 2016, London: DfE.

Dukes, C. and Smith, M. (2009) *Building better behaviour in the early years*. London: Sage.

Foster, D. and Long, R. (2017) *The Pupil Premium: Briefing Paper Number 6700, 12 December 2017*. London: House of Commons Library.

Gabriel, N. (2017) The sociology of early childhood: critical perspectives. London: Sage.

Gambaro, L., Stewart, K. and Waldfogel, J. (2013) A question of quality: do children from disadvantaged backgrounds receive lower quality early years education and care in England? London: Centre for Analysis of Social Exclusion.

Gaunt, C. (2015) *Nurseries face 'chronic' under-funding*. Available at: www.nurseryworld.co.uk/nursery-world/news/1149118/nurseries-chronic-funding (date accessed: 23 January 2018).

GOV.UK (2015) *Policy paper 2010 to 2015 government policy: childcare and early education*. Available at: www.gov.uk/government/publications/2010-to-2015-government-policy-childcare-and-early-education/2010-to-2015-government-policy-childcare-and-early-education#appendix-6-early-years-pupil-premium (date accessed: 1 February 2018).

GOV.UK (2017) *Pupil premium: funding and accountability for schools*. Available at: www.gov.uk/guidance/pupil-premium-information-for-schools-and-alternative-provision-settings (date accessed: 01 February 2018).

GOV.UK (2018a) *Free education and childcare for 2-year-olds if you get benefits*. Available at: www.gov.uk/help-with-childcare-costs/free-childcare-2-year-olds-benefits (date accessed: 17 January 2018).

GOV.UK (2018b) Help paying for childcare. Available at: www.gov.uk/help-with-childcare-costs/free-childcare-and-education-for-2-to-4-year-olds (date accessed: 17 January 2018).

Joseph Rowntree Foundation (JRF) (2017) *Summary report: UK poverty 2017.* York: JRF.

Kennedy, S. (2014) *Child Poverty Act 2010: a short guide.* Available at: http://researchbriefings.parliament.uk/ResearchBriefing/Summary/SN05585 (date accessed: 12 January 2018).

Maslow, A. (1943) A theory of human motivation. *Psychological Review, 50,* 370–396.

Mills, M., Francis, B. and Skelton, C. (2009) Gender policies in Australia and the United Kingdom. In W. Martino, M. Kehler and M. Weaver-Hightower (Eds), *The problem with boys' education: beyond the backlash* (pp. 36–55). London: Routledge.

Mukherji, P. and Dryden, L. (2014) Foundations of early childhood: principles and practice. London: Sage.

National Children's Bureau (NCB) (2015) *Poor beginnings: health inequalities among young children across England.* London: National Children's Bureau.

Pascal, C. and Bertram, T. (2016a) *CREC & HAWWC boys on the early years podcast.* Available at: www.crec.co.uk/announcements/crec-hawwc-boys-on-the-early-years-podcast (date accessed: 10 August 2017).

Pascal, C. and Bertram, T. (2016b) *High Achieving White Working Class (HAWWC) Boys Project: Final Report March 2016.* Birmingham: Centre for Research in Early Childhood.

Sylva, K., Melhuish, E., Sammons, P., Siraj-Blatchford, I. and Taggart, B. (2004*). The effective provision of pre-school education project; findings from the pre-school period.* London: DfES.

Taggart, B., Sylva, K., Melhuish, E., Sammons, P. and Siraj, I. (2015) *Effective pre-school, primary and secondary education project (EPPSE 3–16+).* London: DfE.

Trigg, A. (2004) Deriving the Engel Curve: Pierre Bourdieu and the social critique of Maslow's Hierarchy of Needs. *Review of Social Economy,* 62(3), 393–406.

UNESCO (2017) *Learning to live together.* Available at: www.unesco.org/new/en/social-and-human-sciences/themes/international-migration/glossary/poverty/ (date accessed: 17 January 2018).

Chapter 3

The unique child

Julie Dalton

CHAPTER AIMS

By the end of this chapter you will be able to:

- identify important policies guiding practice around inclusion
- develop a basic awareness of a range of differences which children may present with or develop
- consider a range of strategies for differentiation.

This chapter will seek to define the unique child and to introduce you to the policy around inclusion and how to create an inclusive practice. The first section will introduce Special Educational Needs and Disability (SEND) legislation and look at the new Education, Health and Care (ECH) plans which bring health and education planning together. This will involve an understanding of multi-agency working and understanding the role of parents in making choices. You will be able to distinguish between models of disability and look at issues around labelling and diagnosis. The second section will look specifically at wellbeing for all children; how do we meet individual needs and looking holistically at each child. The final section of the chapter will be looking at the unique child in practice and practical strategies for inclusive practice.

Policy

The key pieces of policy affecting practice with regard to SEND are The Children and Families Act (2014), The Statutory Framework in the EYFS (DfE, 2017), The Equality Act (2010) and the SEND Code of Practice (DfE, 2015).

The Children and Families Act (2014)

In part 3 of this document a change was introduced. This was the creation of Education and Health Care plans (EHC). These plans bring together experts from the fields of health and education and set targets within one document which look holistically at the child. The plans affect children from birth to twenty-five years old. Another change that stemmed from this act was that the local offer for children with SEND has to be published. This should increase parental choice and give everyone an understanding of what is available within the local authority.

The act demanded a focus on positive outcomes and much higher levels of participation in decision making for parents and children. For early years settings the focus is on early identification of issues and this can involve bringing in expertise from outside the setting at any point. Each setting has to identify a person who is the Special Educational Needs Coordinator (SENCO). The SENCO will need to collate evidence and run training for staff to develop understanding around SEN and disability.

Statutory Framework in the EYFS (DfE, 2017)

This framework demands that practitioners provide equality of opportunity and anti-discriminatory practices, ensuring that every child is included and supported (DfE, 2017).

The Equality Act (2010)

Early years settings must promote equality of opportunity and must not discriminate directly or indirectly. The act requires all settings to make reasonable adjustments to include all children.

THINKING ACTIVITY

What might be considered a reasonable adjustment? This might be about access to the building or resources or might include staff training to support individual needs. When you are in placement look for signs of adjustment to include all children.

SEND Code of Practice (2015)

This document says that settings must maintain a culture of high expectations that expects those working with children and young people with SEN or disabilities to include them in all the opportunities available to other children and young people so that they can achieve well. (DfE, 2015, Par 1:31)

Bringing together the EYFS framework and the Code of Practice is the notion of Universal Inclusive Practice. The basis of this idea is seeing every child as a unique child. Practitioners need to build positive relationships with children and to create enabling environments. In early years settings it is recognised that children develop and learn in different ways and at different rates and all learning needs to be differentiated. High quality teaching is based on high expectations for all children. All practitioners must consider the individual needs and interests and stage of development of each child in their care and must use this information to plan a challenging and enjoyable experience for each child for all areas of learning and development.

One of the ways children's needs are met in practice is through the provision of a key person who can tailor the learning and care to meet individual needs. The child's key person also seeks to engage and support parents/carers and help them to engage with specialist support if appropriate.

To create an inclusive practice which will lead to equality of opportunity practitioners are involved from the very beginning of the relationship with the child and their parents/carers. Creating welcoming and secure relationships is based on having respect for difference. Children need equality of access to play, learning and leisure. Children and their families need to be active in making decisions. Staff need to take a proactive approach to reduce barriers and to find access to information and to people.

Case study

Noah is 26 months old and has been at the setting for 8 months. He is settled and appears to have made a firm attachment with his key person who has moved into the 2-year-old room with him. The staff who work alongside Noah have concerns about his language learning and development based on his interactions with staff and children in the setting. Think about what you would expect to happen next and compare your answers with the list below.

Firstly, it is very important that early concerns are recorded and shared with colleagues, the SENCO and parents. Being responsive to concerns and not waiting can have a very positive impact on attainment and behaviour.

A holistic approach needs to be taken which looks at the needs of the child and family as a whole. Information needs to be gathered together and discussed with parents/carers.

The setting needs to consider learning and development needs within and beyond the setting. Specialist advice needs to be sought to back up observations, assessments and checks on progress. Progress needs to be measured carefully against the prime areas of communication and language, physical development and social and emotional development.

Thus from the initial concern a graduated response is needed which involves discussion with carers/parents and which leads to the creation of a targeted plan for this child. The setting might decide to request an EHC needs assessment and this would begin the cycle of: assess, plan, do and review which is continuous.

Development Matters (Early Education, 2012) sums up the role of the setting:

- Observe children as they act and interact in their play, everyday activities and planned activities, and learn from parents about what the child does at home.
- Consider the examples of development in the columns headed Unique Child: Observing what children can do to help identify where the child may be in their own developmental pathway.
- Consider ways to support the child to strengthen and deepen their current learning and development, reflecting on guidance in columns headed Positive Relationships and Enabling Environments. These columns contain some examples of

what practitioners might do to support learning. Practitioners will develop many other approaches in response to the children with whom they work.

Where appropriate, use the developmental statements to identify possible areas in which to challenge and extend the child's current learning and development.

Models of disability

Having considered the legislation and procedures in place it is important to consider how children and families with SEND are viewed and treated in settings and by local authorities. Each locality has to provide and publish the local offer for all children and parents and this is meant to enhance choice and improve decision making. In reality taking an holistic approach to difference of any kind is a challenge because in the UK the dominant model of disability has been the Medical Model. This is a model which is based on seeing any difference in terms of what might need to be 'treated' or 'fixed'. We therefore approach difference by trying to eliminate it and make people the same. We seek medical intervention, medication and treatments to improve the life of the person.

An alternative approach, suggested by groups of people with disability themselves, is the Social Model which looks at difference in terms of what society needs to change to accommodate everyone. This model sees disability as a construct. The person has a difference but society sees that as problematic. When we approach a person we see their difference as a problem and something that the person needs to overcome. The social model sees e.g. the stairs as the problem rather than the wheelchair and suggests that society needs to change to include everyone.

THINKING ACTIVITY

What changes might a setting might need to make in order to apply the social model and be inclusive in terms of access, activity and socialisation? Who decides what is reasonable?

In education the EHC plans bring together both these approaches. The medical needs of the child are considered alongside the reasonable adjustments that the setting can introduce so that the child can access every activity alongside their peers. If a setting is named in the EHC then parents can expect their child to be accepted by that setting and this is seen as one way to increase parental choice. The advantages of having a diagnosis and creating an EHC are that it should increase choice. The label that is applied to the child in this process could be seen as positive if it leads to funding and support but it has to be considered that there is a tension involved in that labelling a child could lead to them being seen as someone with a condition rather than as a unique individual.

To sum up this section it is good to look back to the legislation and what it enshrines in law. One of the purposes of the EYFS is to provide: equality of opportunity and anti-discriminatory practice ensuring that every child is included and supported

(Statutory Framework for EYFS, DfE, 2017, p. 5). This is a big statement and has many implications for practice.

The SEND code of practice 0 to 25 years (2015) highlights a commitment to inclusive education and the progressive removal of barriers to learning and participation in mainstream education. Although these are rights, which are legislated for, the experience of children with disability or difference are determined by the practitioners in each setting they encounter. It is important to consider the experience of every child attending your setting and to judge the quality of provision from the point of view of the child's experience.

In order to prepare you to meet the needs of each individual child and family that you will work with during your placements and your future career the second part of this chapter will introduce you to some of the conditions/differences which children will present with and the final section will offer many practical strategies which you might use to ensure that you are providing an inclusive environment for all.

THINKING ACTIVITY

Think about your current knowledge of any kind of difference. If a new child was joining your setting with e.g. cerebral palsy, would you be thinking, using the social model, about what adaptations might be needed to make the setting inclusive or would you be thinking, using the medical model, about what issues this child will need help with? You might be thinking using both models but remember that the social model focuses more on what the child can do and how to make sure that they are learning and developing alongside their peers whereas the medical model can often focus on what the child is unable to do and what additional support they need.

Range of difficulties and disabilities

In order to prepare to support and include all children attending your setting it is good to have an understanding of a range of difficulties and disabilities. This section aims to give you some basic understanding of, and more importantly some practical strategies around managing, some common issues which children and families may present with.

Attachment disorder

One of the earliest differences which is noticeable in small children is attachment disorder. You will have studied Bowlby's theory and know that not all babies attach positively to their main caregiver and this can mean that they have ongoing issues with attachment which can affect them into adulthood (Bowlby, 1977). It is important to remember that there are a range of reasons why early attachments have not been made. Neglect and abuse are possible causes but we should also consider the possibility of a pre-birth trauma, undiagnosed chronic conditions, such as colic or ear infections, maternal depression and sudden separation from the caregiver due to illness or even death.

What is important to remember is that whatever the cause the condition can improve and positive outcomes are possible. It is vital that you make the link between positive attachments and positive self-esteem and self-worth. As caregivers in your setting you need to be responsive, available and meeting the child's needs to ensure that the child feels safe, capable and worthwhile.

What to look out for:

Children are ... superficially engaging
avoiding eye contact
lacking in the ability to give affection
exhibiting control issues
destructive
lacking in kindness
poor at developing peer relationships
unable to trust
repressing their anger.

It is noticeable straight away that some of these pointers might apply to children with other conditions such as ADHD or autism so being aware can help children and their families to investigate further and to get early intervention in place.

Cerebral palsy

This affects children from just before, during or after birth so it can be recognised and diagnosed early in a child's life. This is a neurological issue which affects muscular movement and control in a variety of ways. The condition can vary also from mild to severe but there are common elements in most cases. Children may have stiff muscles and limited movement or tremor and shaky movements. Poor coordination is common and fine motor movements are limited. Speech is often affected either with slurring or scanning (long pauses and breathy monotone voice). Hearing and vision need intervention often and some children favour one eye or have double vision. Some form of seizures are common but these again cover the whole spectrum. Between 30–50% of people with the disorder will have some issues with cognitive elements such as: attention span, memory, comprehension and problem solving. It is important to remember however that over half of the people with this condition learn well and do not have cognitive difficulties.

Visual impairment

Children are considered to have a visual impairment if they require special arrangements to access the physical environment and/or the curriculum. If a child's vision is fully corrected by wearing glasses or contact lenses, then this is not classed as an impairment.

Blind children need tactile and/or audio methods of learning and the involvement of a specialist teacher of the blind is recommended. Partially sighted children could have issues with their near or distance vision. Some may have peripheral distortion, not be able to see 3D images or not be able to judge movement and speed. Size, colour, contrast, position and lighting can make a big difference to how much children can see but this is all individual. Many children with sight problems have other health issues and disabilities too. This is called comorbidity and often makes diagnosis and planning more difficult.

Hearing impairment

It is important to remember that deaf children cover the full range of abilities and hearing impairment does not affect learning per se. The type of hearing loss can be permanent, mild, moderate, severe or profound. Hearing loss can also be temporary and due to a condition like glue ear. It is estimated by the National Institute of Health and Clinical Excellence (Nice, 2008, cited in National Deaf Children's Society, 2015, p. 7) that 20% of children in reception class might have glue ear at any one time and they could be missing between 20 and 50% of what is being said. This temporary condition causes difficulties in hearing on one side or working out where the sound is coming from. Children will find it hard to hear when there is background noise or more than one person speaking. Often they will have to have instructions repeated and may appear reluctant to join in.

Children may arrive in your setting without having been identified as having a hearing loss, or they might acquire a permanent hearing loss during the early years. It is therefore important for staff to look out for any of the possible signs of deafness. The following may indicate a potential hearing loss:

- Does not come when called, watches faces/lips intently, constantly says 'What?', does not follow simple instructions or follows instructions incorrectly.
- Watches what others are doing before doing it themselves and appears to watch and follow peers rather than hearing instructions directly.
- Talks either too loudly or too softly.
- Appears inattentive or as though daydreaming.
- Makes little or no contribution to group discussions, e.g. during story time.
- Rubs ears or complains about not being able to hear.
- Tires easily and becomes frustrated easily.
- Seems socially isolated and less involved in play with other children.

Mental health issues

Until recently very young children were diagnosed with behavioural difficulties rather than specific mental health issues but now there are more instances of children receiving a specific diagnosis for depression or anxiety rather than just noting that their behaviour is unusual. Educational establishments and systems however may still be more comfortable discussing children's wellbeing or behaviour rather than considering their mental health.

The United Nation Convention on the Rights of the Child (1989) states that 'All children have the right to good health including mental health'. It is important to consider that the term 'mental health' can be associated only with issues and negatives and there is still a stigma associated with the phrase. It is a more positive approach to consider that we all have mental health as we have physical health and a definition of what good mental health means to the individual should be our starting point. Positive mental health allows us to make and maintain relationships, to build resilience, deal with transitions and cope with stress.

Cefai and Camilleri (2015) estimate that about 20% of school children experience SEBD in the course of one year and this includes children with ADHD, behavioural issues, anxiety and depression. Since children with SEBD are most vulnerable to exclusion, substance abuse, violence and criminality, it is vital that these mental health issues are noted early and that children are given the support that they require to work towards the positive definition of mental health that will allow them to progress and manage. Harraldsson et al. (2016) agree and consider that 'promoting young children's mental health is an investment for the future' (p 386). Their article looks at the different facets of wellbeing. Emotional wellbeing means that a person can be calm, cheerful and satisfied with their life. Social wellbeing includes feeling integrated, a sense of belonging and being accepted. Psychological wellbeing allows children to experience positive attitudes to themselves and to form trusting and warm relationships with others.

Autism/Autistic Spectrum Disorder/Asperger syndrome

The Autistic Spectrum describes a lifelong neurodevelopmental condition which affects people differently. This is not a disease or an illness and there is no 'cure'. All people on the spectrum share some characteristics but each person will be affected in a different way. Some people with ASD also have mental health issues or other conditions. Anxiety affects many people on the spectrum because the condition is anxiety provoking. Signs of anxiety should be looked for and treated promptly.

There are approximately 1 in 100 children affected in the UK and more boys seem to be affected than girls but research is ongoing. Social communication and language issues are usual across the spectrum. Early identification is important and as young as 9 months it is possible to see the effects of the disorder. Does the child respond to his/her name? If there is no response to the name or to being spoken to this is a cause for further investigation. Children with ASD avoid eye contact; older children describe making eye contact as painful. If children do not make eye contact or show enjoyment during game playing then again this needs to be noted. ASD can make children obsessive in their play and activity; they often want to repeat the same activity over and over for hours and become very distressed when encouraged to change or share. All children enjoy movement but the disorder can lead to repeated movements such as hand flapping, rocking and head banging.

There are signs of the spectrum visible from infancy but most children start having investigations between 18 months and diagnosis is usual by the age of 3. Things to look out for in practice would be:

- Hand flapping which is seen in all children up to the age of 3 but would be more often and still occurring after 3.
- Walking on tiptoes; this again is usual behaviour in infants but would persist and be common practice if the child has ASD.
- Fussiness, tantrums and screaming in public places is a feature of early childhood behaviour but in children on the spectrum it is caused by overstimulation and

sensory overload. The tantrum is not ended by giving the child something he/she desires and the response is uncontrollable and long lasting.

- Biting and aggression are outlets for frustration at not being able to communicate well. Speech milestones are not met and some children are totally non-verbal.
- Echolalia is repetition of sounds/words without understanding of meaning and this is a common feature. Children simply repeat a word or phrase without needing a response.
- Another common issue is hyper or hypo sensitivity. This occurs across the senses and leads to problems with food and clothing. A label inside clothing can be painful and a cause of distress and children may refuse to eat unless the food is not touching, aligned in a certain way and of a particular texture.
- Sleep problems are common across the spectrum and a lack of rest can impact on all interactions and cause family difficulties.

Asperger syndrome is also referred to as high functioning autism because people with Asperger syndrome are of average or above average intelligence. They do not have the learning disabilities that many autistic people have, but they may have specific learning difficulties. They have fewer problems with speech but may still have difficulties with understanding and processing language. Often people with this condition find social and emotional interaction to be difficult and making and retaining friends can be a challenge.

Attention Deficit Hyperactivity Disorder (ADHD)

Another condition which can go on into adulthood and which has some similarities with ASD, this is characterised by a lack of attention and ability to focus. The common misconception is that hyperactivity is always present and that children will be constantly moving and fidgeting. It is possible to have ADD without the hyperactivity and for some this is more difficult to diagnose and children are just seen as unresponsive or dreamy. Similar to ASD, children do not respond when called and fail to follow instructions. Often children are labelled as difficult or naughty as their responses are often impulsive and they fail to recognise the consequences of their actions. ADHD makes it difficult for people to inhibit their spontaneous responses – responses that can involve everything from movement to speech to attentiveness. Some children with ADHD are hyperactive, while others sit quietly—with their attention miles away. Some put too much focus on a task and have trouble shifting it to something else. Others are only mildly inattentive, but overly impulsive.

The three primary characteristics of ADHD are inattention, hyperactivity and impulsivity. The signs and symptoms a child with attention deficit disorder has depend on which characteristics predominate. Because we expect very young children to be easily distractible and hyperactive, it is the impulsive behaviours—the dangerous climb, the blurted insult—that often stand out in children of pre-school age with ADHD. By age four or five, though, most children have learned how to pay attention to others, to sit quietly when instructed to and not to say everything that pops into their heads. So by the time children reach school age, those with ADHD stand out in all three behaviours: inattentiveness, hyperactivity and impulsivity.

There are signs for each strand which should be noted during observation:

- *Inattention*. The child has trouble staying focused and is easily bored and distracted. The child appears not to listen and respond when spoken to. They have difficulty following instructions and paying attention to detail. Often careless mistakes are made.
- *Hyperactivity*. Children frequently lose or misplace their belongings. They constantly move or fidget. They have difficulty staying seated, playing quietly or relaxing. They move around, run and climb inappropriately with no sense of risk. Children with ADHD may talk excessively and be short tempered.
- *Impulsivity*. Children act without thinking and there is no notion of consequence. They may blurt out or guess an answer often without waiting for the full question. They often intrude inappropriately into others' conversations or games and interrupt. If upset, they may be violent or have a temper tantrum which they are unable to control.

It can be seen from this list that there are some similar responses to those with ASD and it is necessary for the setting to seek expert opinion and diagnosis from an educational psychologist and/or other specialist support services to identify and strategise around the conditions identified.

Foetal Alcohol Syndrome (FAS)

Some of the characteristics of this disorder are the same as those for ADHD and this must be ruled out if there are no additional clear means of diagnosis. This condition is neurological and leads to developmental and growth differences and sometimes to characteristic facial features (narrow, small eyes; small head, thin upper lip and a smooth area between the nose and lips). During pregnancy if alcohol enters the baby's system via the placenta it can affect growth and development. Some of the effects are time limited e.g. the facial features are finely honed during weeks 6 to 9 of gestation so it is more likely to see the facial features of FAS if the mother drank consistently through this stage of the pregnancy. Effects on the baby's organs are more likely if alcohol was present during the first trimester but effects on the brain and spinal cord are felt throughout the whole term.

FAS leads to learning disabilities, poor organisation, a lack of inhibition, difficulties with fine motor skills (writing/drawing), balance problems, and attention and hyperactivity issues. The syndrome was first identified in the 1970s and since then research has developed with the identification of Foetal Alcohol Spectrum Disorder (FASD) which is an umbrella term to cover all the effects of alcohol on growth and development.

It is vital to get an early diagnosis because FASD can lead to issues with: hearing; weight and height, hormonal disorders, epilepsy, liver damage; kidney and heart defects, mouth, teeth and facial changes and a weakened immune system.

Later signs which often do not occur until school age are:

- difficulty with group social interaction
- egocentricity
- failure to learn from the consequences of their actions

- hyperactivity and poor attention
- inability to grasp instructions
- lack of appropriate social boundaries (such as over friendliness with strangers)
- learning difficulties
- mixing reality and fiction
- poor coordination.
- problems with language
- poor problem solving and planning
- poor short-term memory.

It is clear from this list that there are many issues which are similar to ADHD and to ASD so a correct diagnosis and EHC plan is needed as early as possible.

Down's Syndrome

This is caused by an extra chromosome and typically leads to characteristic facial features and some form of learning difficulty but each person is affected differently. Having a learning difficulty means that support will be needed for learning but does not mean that the person cannot learn. Often diagnosed at or soon after birth this is a condition which affects 1 in every 1000 babies on average so around 750 babies in the UK every year.

Summary

The second section of this chapter has introduced some of the more common differences which make children unique and has given you some basic information about how to notice and act on observations to ensure that every unique child is supported and challenged to develop effectively. You as a practitioner are not meant to be an expert in any of these differences but it is necessary to have awareness and to be noticing behaviours and/or characteristics which need to be shared with colleagues, the SENCO and parents/carers so that everyone is working together in the best interests of the child.

In the final section of this chapter we will consider practical strategies to ensure the creation of a universal, inclusive practice. The chapter will reference sources of information and expertise and reiterate the importance of the code of practice and utilising EHC plans to best support parents in their choice of suitable provision.

This section is split into awareness raising, policy and practice and practical strategies.

Awareness raising

Awareness raising is essential to make practitioners notice and act on behaviours or characteristics that come to light during observations and working with the child. Awareness raising can be through a training programme or cascaded through the setting from experts within or without of the workplace. It is possible to access information online about the needs of children with specific differences but it is important to check the reliability and validity of the website visited and also to note that some are written from the point of view of the medical model of disability.

Policy and practice

To meet the needs of all children at all times practitioners need to refer to the Code of Practice and the EYFS. Practitioner toolkits are available for SEND and for individual differences. Each setting will refer to national policies and have their own internal policies on inclusion which every staff member needs to refer to. The SENCO in each setting is responsible for collating information, planning resources and staffing, and meeting and reviewing progress with parents/carers and multi-agency colleagues. The EHC plans created for some children will set targets specific to the child. These plans must be regularly and meaningfully reviewed and updated.

There are many sources of expertise available to local authorities and the utilisation of speech and language therapists, educational psychologists and ASD outreach staff has to be coordinated and followed up by the staff in each setting to ensure that the child's needs are being supported. It is important to remember that within each setting there will be experienced colleagues who have a wealth of expertise so sharing and disseminating information and strategies is an important means of making every member of staff aware. The other resource which needs to be drawn upon is the knowledge of parents. Carers/parents know their children and the setting has to ensure that parents/carers are included in every decision and that their voices are heard in meetings and reviews.

Practical strategies

This concluding section will look at some overall strategies in supporting the learning and development of all children within a universal, inclusive practice and it will suggest further training and resources which will be useful for continuous professional development.

Meeting the needs of an individual child might be accomplished by using simple, practical strategies such as providing extra time for completion of tasks or extra time to explain the requirements of an activity. It may be necessary to allow longer to observe certain children and their targets may need to be based on smaller steps of progress. Paperwork often has to be edited to record the new goals and reviews may be needed more frequently. It is important to remember that all goals set must be challenging and our planning for every unique child is based on a culture of high expectations. Working with parents/carers to support every unique child is imperative and the voice of the child; their likes/dislikes is vital to planning for them. The child themselves needs to be part of the target setting and review process.

Training

There are many training opportunities available for Continuing Professional Development (CPD) and some are suggested here as useful for mainstream practice. Paediatric first aid is useful to deal with accidents and emergencies but also the physical aspects of conditions as mentioned earlier in the chapter such as epilepsy, fainting or choking. There is a mental health first aid course available and training through Children and Adolescents' Mental Health Services (CAMHS) to increase awareness about wellbeing issues. ASD awareness raising is informative and there are specialist training courses available for safe handling and restraint under Team Teach. This would be useful for those staff working one to one with a child on the spectrum but all members of staff would benefit from having this training to deescalate any incidence of a loss of control as was highlighted in the sections on ASD and ADHD.

There are many technological adaptations to assist children and to enable their learning and development. Lots of free accessible tools are built into Microsoft programs and then there are pieces of software and hardware which can help. Children may benefit from an accessible mouse in the shape of a joystick or a head based mouse which allows them to work hands free. There are specific programs to help with communication and language. Visual impairment can be aided by the use of large print versions and different contrast between text and background. There are screen reading programs which speak a version of what is on the screen and when children are older they may benefit from braille text which is now widely available.

Sign language is used by some children with a hearing impairment and basic sign language can be built into the whole setting so that children feel included and are able to communicate with their hearing peers. Makaton is a different signed language which is used by children who are non- verbal for a variety of reasons.

Some specialist programmes such as Picture Exchange Communication System (PECS) allow children to communicate without speech and can be tailored to each child's needs and interests. Often a visual timetable is useful to allow children with ASD and Down's Syndrome to prepare for transitions during the day. A sensory room or some sensory resources can aid learning for a range of children and it is essential to have somewhere quiet and calm for children to recover from losses of control or over stimulation.

This chapter has outlined the policies governing inclusive practice and how practitioners can put these into practice. The different models of disability were outlined and it is good to remind ourselves never to see the condition before the individual child. The behaviour that accompanies some conditions is negative but this doesn't mean that we should see the child in a negative light. The practitioner's role will be to help the child to manage their behaviour and develop strategies to cope and change the behaviour where possible. It is essential to base our practice on a culture of high expectations for the learning and development of all children in the setting and to share and disseminate expertise so that everyone is aware of best practice.

THINKING ACTIVITY

In any setting children are grouped together in ages and stages but that does not mean that they are all the same. During your course you will have been reflecting on yourself as a learner and considering whether you need additional support for any particular area of the curriculum or with your academic skills. Think about what makes you unique not just in your learning but in your personality. The notion of each child being unique helps practitioners to take a holistic approach to assessing, observing and supporting each child that they work with.

References

Bowlby, J. (1977) The making and breaking of affectional bonds. 1. Aetiology and psychopathology in the light of attachment theory. *The British Journal of Psychiatry* 130, 201–210.

Cefai, C. and Camilleri, L. (2015) A healthy start: promoting mental health and wellbeing in the early primary school years. *Emotional and Behavioural Difficulties,* 20 (2), 133–152.

Children and Families Act (2014) The Stationery Office. Available from: www.legislation.gov.uk/ukpga/2014/6/contents/enacted

DfE (2015) *SEND Code Of Practice 0–2 years.* Available at: www.gov.uk/government/publications/send-code-of-practice-0-to-25

DfE (2017). *Statutory framework for the early years foundation stage. Setting the standards for learning, development and care for children from birth to five.* London: DfE.

Early Education (2012). *Development Matters.* Available at: www.foundationyears.org.uk/files/2012/03/Development-Matters-FINAL-PRINT-AMENDED.pdf

Equality Act (2010) Available at: www.legislation.gov.uk/ukpga/2010/15/contents

Haraldsson, K., Isaksson, P. and Eriksson, M. (2016) 'Happy when they arrive, happy when they go home' – focusing on promoting children's mental health creates a sense of trust at preschools. *Early Years,* 37 (4), 386–399. DOI: 10.1080/09575146.2016.1191442

National Deaf Children's Society (2015) *Supporting the achievement of hearing impaired children in early years' settings for professionals working with children aged 0 to 4.* National Sensory Impairment Partnership funded by DfE.

National Institute of Health and Clinical Excellence (2008) *Surgical Management of Otitis Media with Effusion in Children.* London: NICE.

SEND Tool. (n.d.) Available at: https://councilfordisabledchildren.org.uk/sites/default/files/field/attachemnt/early-years-toolkit-merged.pdfkit

United Nations Convention on the Rights of the Child (1989) Available at: www.childrensrights.ie/childrens-rights-ireland/un-convention-rights-child

Chapter 4

Listening and responding to children's voice

Wayne Bailey, Judith Hunter and Frances Marsden

CHAPTER AIMS

By the end of this chapter you will be able to:

- know the principles of human rights and the UN (1989) Convention on the Rights of the Child
- consider ways of listening to and responding to children
- be aware of ways of working with children to enable their voices to be heard
- consolidate your learning through case studies that apply theory to practice.

Introduction

This chapter will help you, the student, to understand theories and models of empowerment concerning the voice of children in the early years sector. It will encourage you to evaluate the complexities of international, political, socio-economic, ethical and cultural implications within the context of the United Nations Convention on the Rights of the Child (UN, 1989). The chapter offers you the student the opportunity to develop your understanding of children's capacity to express their voice, through case study analysis applying theory to practice. The aim of the chapter is to help you to work towards becoming an advanced practitioner and improve your effectiveness in responding to the needs of children, and to encourage you to participate meaningfully to influence policy and practice in an early years context. Each case study will enhance your understanding of voice by showcasing how specific settings are encouraging children and young people's active participation to influence policy and practice in a range of settings. The case studies explore the significance of voice and identify appropriate responses to key and topical issues. It is envisaged that the case studies will allow you to become more effective in responding to the needs of children and help to ensure that they have a voice. Following each case study, you will find a reflective task, an activity or questions that will enable further understanding of ways of engaging and listening to children. Each case study is based on small-scale research projects undertaken by students at the University of Huddersfield.

The voice of children

In the UK there is a call for children's voices to be heard and for adults to find ways to seek their opinions in matters that affect their lives. One definition of voice comes from 'determining what constitutes the interests of children and young people's views being actively sought, listened to, taken seriously and acted upon by services and agencies responsible for their welfare' Office of the High Commissioner for Human Rights (OHCHR, 1989, p. 4) cited in Czerniawski and Kidd (2011, p. 49). Throughout this chapter the case studies will guide you through ways you can achieve this.

Article 12 of the UN Convention on the Rights of the Child ensures we ascertain the wishes and feelings of the child which is also required under the welfare checklist of the Children Act 1989. If children are to act as 'participatory citizens' in a true democracy (as opposed to one where rights can be constrained by factors such as age, and presumption of lack of competence) they must be listened to. Only in this way can children be 'subjects' who act in their own right and not the 'objects of concern' whose 'best interests' and 'welfare' are interpreted on their behalf by adults (Roche, 1999 cited in O'Quigley, 2000, p. 1). In order to ensure we truly listen to children we need to find appropriate ways of communicating with them effectively. O'Quigley (2000, p. iv) states 'Good communication is more likely to occur if adults see children's abilities and competencies as being different from rather than lesser than adults.' It may also be helpful to remember that children view the world differently to adults. Professor Sir Albert Aynsley-Green (Children's Commissioner for England, from 2005 to 2009) continues to act as an advocate for children and young people, to ensure their interests are considered in decisions about public policy. He commented at a student conference in Huddersfield University (2018) that:

Children and young people matter – to families and to society. Quite simply, they are our nation's most precious resource. As well as being citizens in their own right today, they are the workers and parents of the future on whom our prosperity will depend.

Considering this view, we need to think carefully how to help children develop their own ideas and views and show them that they can and should be listened to, as Sir Al suggests there could be serious consequences for our future if we do not develop children into contributing citizens of the future.

As a student, and later when you become a qualified practitioner, you will have the power to assist children in having a voice, it is important to ensure you use that power wisely and effectively when employed in the children's and young people's workforce. Qvortrup (1994) suggests that children are people in their own right and as human beings they hold human rights. Children should have an opinion in matters that affect them; they have the right of participation in making decisions that may affect their lives, this is important for you to remember. Our human rights are the basic things we need in order to live with dignity, develop and reach our potential. Basic needs such as food, housing and health care and the right to express ourselves, hold religious beliefs and be free from violence and abuse are all very important. We all have these rights no matter who we are, what we are like or what we do. Nobody has to earn human rights – we are entitled to our rights simply because we are human. We all rely on our human rights all of the time – mostly without knowing it. It is only when someone violates our rights that we realise how much we need them and it is the UK government who has a responsibility to make sure that people's rights can be accessed, are respected and can be enjoyed by providing legislation and policy to protect our human rights.

Children and young people need special rights because they are relatively more vulnerable compared to adults. The UNCRC (1989) brings together children's human rights into one international convention. It is an international agreement across the world which sets out the rights of children from birth until 18 and has been in existence for almost 30 years following its adoption by the UN General Committee in 1989. It was ratified in 1991 and came into force within the UK in 1992. The UK government continues its commitment to pay 'due regard' to the Convention when new policy is made and legislation is proposed such as Children Act 1989, Children Act 2004, Every Child Matters (DfES, 2003) and policy for 0–19-year-olds set out in the Labour Government's (2007) Children's Plan (DCSF, 2007) and the Children's Plan one year on (DCSF, 2008).

The UNCRC itself consists of 54 articles, with some articles referring directly to the voice of children and young people. For example, Article 12 gives children the right to express their views freely and to be heard – the right to a 'voice'. However, as Lundy (2007, p. 929) argues, there are 'barriers to the implementation' of the Article and an alternative model for conceptualising it may be required. Specifically, if Article 12 is to be implemented successfully it is necessary to consider:

- Space: Children must be given the opportunity to express a view
- Voice: Children must be facilitated to express their views
- Audience: The view must be listened to
- Influence: The view must be acted upon, as appropriate.

The UNCRC rights perspective embraces children's participation and acknowledges that children have ideas about their lives and what directly affects them, they have a view of their world. It will become your responsibility to accommodate children to express their views, listen to them and act appropriately when you become a practitioner.

THINKING ACTIVITY

Access the UNCRC (1989) at https://www.unicef.org.uk and locate the 54 Articles.

Compile a list of Articles that you think are relevant for the children in your care. Why is this? Share your ideas.

In the statutory guidance *Listening to and involving children and young people* (Department for Education, 2014) schools are 'strongly encouraged to pay due regard to the Convention' and attention is drawn, in particular, to Article 12 and to the value of 'pupil voice'. Significant progress appears to have been made with 'student voice' being extensively promoted and implemented. Examples include the UNICEF Rights Respecting Schools initiative which is widely supported and has been shown to have a positive impact (Covell and McNeil, 2010; Sebba and Robinson, 2010).

Case study

Aimee's research focused on play areas and resources and investigates how children in a reception class are offered the opportunity to use their voice to discuss how they feel about play. Her research emphasises the importance of the UNCRC and makes specific reference to Article 31 which covers play and suggests that children need the time and space to be able to play and be creative (Kilvington and Wood, 2016). A number of themes were evident in Aimee's data including how and in what ways do children play, what influences their play and where do they play? Aimee's data suggested that children appeared to have set ideas of what boys and girls should play with. The research indicated that the toys had become gendered – the toys were either for girls, or for boys. Within the setting where this research takes place, there were limited numbers of toys that were gender neutral (Kilvington and Wood, 2016). There was a suggestion that parents and other adults had an impact on what children played with, how they play and who with. Trains and trucks were bought for boys, dolls and princesses for girls (Servos, Dewar, Bosacki and Coplan, 2017). Play was used as a mechanism for voice, as the children could choose any toy to play with, could play in any part of the play area, with any child they wanted to play with. However, Aimee makes the point that gender stereotypes linked to play can stifle children's voices in many ways in terms of what they play, how they play and who with.

THINKING ACTIVITY

Why is it important for the staff to be aware of the UNCRC? What information would you provide for staff as a guide when purchasing new resources and toys for the setting?

Undertake an audit of the toys and resources in your setting. Make a list of the resources that show a clear gender bias, highlighting whether each is male or female specific. Make a second list of resources that clearly have no gender bias. Consider how you present these resources to children. From the information gathered, how would you advise parents on buying toys for their child?

School councils are near universal, even if their effectiveness is variable (Davies, Williams, Yamashita and Ko Man-Hing, 2006; Whitty and Wisby, 2007). Participation is also widely identified as a means of evidencing school improvement (Bragg, 2007; Rudduck and Flutter, 2000). Other articles which are important to the voice of children and young people include Article 5 which refers to helping children to understand and exercise their rights and Article 13 which refers to using appropriate media for the children to communicate.

THINKING ACTIVITY

Access and read Articles 12 and 13 and consider ways in which your place-ment addresses these. Make a list of the ways the staff team empower children's voices to be heard. Critically reflect on how this was achieved.

As a student, and later when you become a qualified practitioner you will need to consider how you bring all of this into the early years profession. As you work with young children and babies you will begin to understand how you can build a rapport with a child and tune into their needs by sensitively listening to them, using your ears and eyes to pick up body language and expression cues that tell you a great deal about how a non-verbal child is feeling. If you are interested in truly listening to a child's per-spective, you will be motivated to investigate with the child to find out how they feel.

You will attempt to interpret and understand their lives in order to provide them with the opportunity to experience some element of control over their lives by giving them the confidence to 'voice' their ideas and thoughts. Examples might include de-ciding what activities to engage in, or when and what to eat (Green and Hill, 2005).

THINKING ACTIVITY

Let us think about 'listening' to babies and young children. Reflect on what is meant by 'listening' to babies and young children. Observe practitioners during mealtimes. Make a list of the key points you observed.

As you develop as an advanced practitioner, it will be your responsibility to plan for op-portunities to give the children in your care the time and space to express their voice. You will need to consider the values, approaches and practices of everyday work with young children to establish spaces and places for children's rights and participation to develop. It is important that you remember that children have voices, you are not 'giving them a voice'. It is vitally important that you consider how you can build participation and to encourage contribution from children. You need to think about how you listen to them, perceive them and how you act on what they tell you. You need to be aware that children may not be used to being taken seriously, or being listened to (Westcott and Littleton, 2005) therefore building a rapport and trusting relationship with them will be vital.

Lundy (2007:5) points out that it is unreasonable to expect children to become 'respon-sible participating citizens at 16, 18 or 21,' they need to be given the opportunity to learn how to make decisions by working with adults from a young age. There are clearly positive reasons for listening to children, but as Woodhead and Faulkner (2008, p. 35) comment 'respect for children's status as social actors does not diminish adult responsibilities'. Children will remain vulnerable and need protecting and safeguarding from harm. Lansdown (1994) suggests society sees children as vulnerable and powerless so when working with children you need to consider how to protect them from being manipulated and show them respect for their views and opinions. If we consider children to be agentic rights bearing individuals, who have the right to be consulted, have freedom of speech, have their opinions considered and have access to information about their own lives and what affects them, then we recognise children as participants in society (Sorin, 2003).

Case study

Tom investigated the role of a school council as a voice mechanism within a primary school. Specifically, he wanted to find out how teachers' support effective management of school councils and how they support children, within a school council, to give the children agency. Tom drew on the concept of 'multivocality voice' within society which is simply defined as 'many voices' explaining that a notable example would be school councils which help to support and combine various children's views on a particular topic (Robinson and Taylor, 2013).

Tom's research uncovered issues of 'power', he related to the work of Cox and Robinson-Pant (2005) who identified a 'power dynamic' within school councils. Tom suggested that on some occasions ideas were dismissed without due consideration appearing to be given to them.

Having a voice was clearly important to Tom's participants. They expressed enjoyment and pleasure as they were able to make decisions that directly impacted upon their school life and often discussed 'visible changes' within the school which they could see on a daily basis. In line with Burnitt and Gunter (2013) Tom's work suggested that school councils provided a platform for children to express opinions, develop and to have a voice on important school matters.

THINKING ACTIVITY

What is the key purpose of a School Council? Who are the members of the School Council? How often does the School Council meet? If possible, observe a School Council meeting in progress. Who leads the meeting? Who sets the agenda/topics for discussion? Share your findings with the group.

Having observed a School Council meeting, who has the 'power'? Are the children's voices heard? What evidence do you have to support this? If possible, find out what changes have been implemented throughout the school as a result of the School Council.

Theoretical approaches for listening to voice

Hart's ladder of participation

Considering Hart's (1992) model will help you to investigate, and to begin to understand, how society, and adults in particular, can aid or hinder the degree to which children participate in their own lives. Hart displays children's participation as a ladder which starts at the bottom with little or no participation and moves to the top where children initiate and share decision making. The top five rungs of the ladder

Table 4.1 Hart's ladder of participation

Rung 8 is child initiated; they have shared decision making with adults. Children incorporate adult support into their projects, to work successfully together.

Rung 7 is child initiated and directed. Children decide a project and carry it out with adults providing supportive conditions. Adults respond to the children's needs by listening and responding to them appropriately.

Rung 6 is adult initiated; shared decisions are made with children. Projects are initiated by adults but children share in the decision making, they have a voice which is listened to.

Rung 5 is consulted with the child and the child is informed. Projects are designed and run by adults; children understand this but know their opinions are treated seriously.

Rung 4 is assigned but informed. This is the basic participatory level. Children understand the intention of what they are asked to do, they know they are involved and they agree to be involved.

Rung 3 is tokenism. Children are told they have a voice but have no choice in how they express it. There is no participation as adults appear to give the children a voice but children find it difficult to engage with adult processes.

Rung 2 is decoration. Children have no idea about the reason for their inclusion, this could be considered as adults using or manipulating children.

Rung 1 is manipulation. Child has no understanding of the action/issues; adults use children's ideas without further involvement of them.

Adapted from (Hart, 1992)

have varying degrees of participation for children, the lower three rungs are considered to not have any participation. Table 4.1 shows Hart's ladder.

As you develop as a practitioner, your aim should be to listen to children, to encourage them to explore the spectrum of participation from the agentic perspective of the child. You need to ensure that they have the right to express their views freely and to have their views be given due weight in accordance with age and maturity (Lundy, 2007). This is not easy, you will need to adopt a calm and approachable manner in listening and respecting the opinions of individual children, empowering and encouraging their participation. Developing a participatory ethos within your early years setting, and encouraging children to engage in free flow play and exploration is one way of ensuring the child's voice is heard alongside keeping them physically safe. Another way would be to ensure that children's participation permeates the daily routine within the setting. 'It is important to remember that children who speak do not always say what they mean, as a listener you need to develop a skill set that enables you to hear between the lines' (Davie, Upton and Varma, 1996, p. 95). If children cannot or decide not to speak, it does not mean the child has nothing to say; you need to remember that the child has the right to be heard even if it is apparent that something is preventing them from doing so.

Spyrou (2016, p. 3) acknowledges that listening better includes hearing silence and that silence is not neutral or empty. It is important that you are patient and that you take time to try to interpret the silence. As you build your experience as a practitioner you will develop both a reflective and reflexive approach and this will help you to decode the silence. Moosa-Mitha (2005) suggests that simply having a voice is not enough and that it is equally important to also be heard in order to have a presence in society, but listening should not be tokenistic by nature, all this will do is reinforce the power balance in favour of the adult (Brooker, 2011).

Case study

Fatima's research explores the voice mechanisms utilised within a reception class. The research focused on the use of circle time as a mechanism to give a voice to children with English as an additional language (EAL). Specifically, she was interested in how effective circle time was at enabling children's voices to be heard and listened to, whilst taking account of the barriers that children with EAL face during circle time. The research highlighted that circle time enabled the children to be heard, and in doing so promote honesty and respect. Fatima suggested that children with EAL can experience quiet periods whilst they adjust to their environments, particularly if they have language difficulties (Graf, 2011), with some of the children being reluctant to say anything as they lacked confidence. The research also suggested the need to respect and to recognise children's silence (Clark and Moss, 2011), particularly staff in settings, and the need to consider various meanings and a means of interpreting the silence.

As a result of language difficulties, this research highlighted a lack of participation in circle time; it was suggested that key elements of Article 12 of the UNCRC (1989) should be considered if practitioners were to use circle time as a mechanism for voice for children with EAL. Fatima suggested that staff at the setting encouraged the children to be open about issues by creating an atmosphere that was happy and relaxed and that this fostered respect (Tangen and Spooner-Lane, 2008). It was made clear that it was important to use a range of mechanisms that did not require oral communication (as well as circle time) in order to benefit children with EAL such as mood boards, mood walls, show and tell, and age appropriate surveys for example.

Fatima draws a number of interesting conclusions, specifically that 'voice' does not only involve giving children with EAL a voice in the classroom and enabling them to speak. To be successful, practitioners need to engage in critical reflection, interpretation and representation (Clark and Moss, 2011).

THINKING ACTIVITY

Observe the different ways in which circle time is used. How can circle time be used as an effective tool for listening to children? List the skills required of a practitioner in order to run a successful circle time session? Complete a SWOT analysis of your own skills. Devise an action plan to enhance your own skills.

You have been asked by the class teacher to take a story session for children with English as an Additional Language (EAL) using the children's favourite book, Monkey Puzzle by Julia Donaldson (2000). Produce a detailed activity plan that clearly shows how you will involve children with EAL. What resources will you use and why? How does this activity provide evidence of listening to the children's voices? Implement the activity and ask the teacher to provide constructive feedback.

THINKING ACTIVITY

How could you promote children's agency, voice and contributions in your practice?
Who controls the spaces and materials in the setting?
How can children participate in making choices and being heard?
How important is reflection and reflexivity in this process?

As you gain confidence in understanding your role through observation, observing and being observant (Dubiel, 2016), you will begin to appreciate the need to listen and respect the opinions of the children in your care. It is important to recognise that there is no one 'universal child' that stands for all children and that children's experiences are multiple and varied (James and Prout, 1990). A practitioner who values children's perspectives and wishes to understand their 'lived experiences' will be motivated to find out more about how children understand, interpret, negotiate and feel about their daily lives (Green and Hill, 2005, p. 3). It is paramount that students and practitioners are committed to not only providing opportunities for children's voices to be heard, but also to listen to what they are saying.

Being aware of how settings and organisations respond to children's voice and the ways in which this occurs will be beneficial for both the children and your own professional practice. In addition, it may highlight areas for further development for the setting's staff team.

As explored earlier in the chapter, you will now have a clearer understanding of the UNCRC and how it can empower you as a practitioner to develop ways of listening to children. Gaining knowledge and understanding of the Articles can 'inform and enhance your practice, shape personal thinking and positively influence provision for children' (Brownhill, 2014, p. 6). Increasing and improving the ways in which you and practitioners listen to children's voices can only take place with hard work, dedication and commitment from those who embrace learning along with a feeling of empowerment.

The Mosaic Approach

The Mosaic Approach to listening to young children devised by Clark and Moss (2001) encompasses a range of different tools or activities that can be used 'with' and 'by' children in order to gain their perspective. Children have the capacity to act independently, to make choices about the things they do and to express their own ideas. Try and be creative in the way you plan and arrange resources and activities for children. Children are more capable than you think. For example, the individual pieces of the Mosaic Approach include: observation, photographs, book making, tours and map making. These may sound quite complicated as methods of listening to children, but if planned well and the activity is explained clearly to the children, they will amaze you with their results. For example, consider asking the children about their favourite places to play at nursery or school. Often the teacher may ask the children to share their ideas and talk about these places during carpet time. This is a good example of listening to children's voices. How different would this listening be if this was followed by an activity where the children had cameras and were encouraged to take photographs of their favourite places? This could then be followed with the children being able to print the photographs and share their feelings by telling the rest of the group why this is their favourite place. Perhaps they could make a display or compile a book to show parents and visitors. The learning potential from this simple activity not only empowers the children's voice, it encourages listening and in addition offers many valuable learning experiences. A fun activity has empowered the children to express their voice and share it with others.

Understanding the different ways in which it is possible to empower children's voices in early years settings can only enhance your own professional practice. Observing practitioners and gaining understanding of how this can be achieved is key. Using any aspect/method from the Mosaic Approach or even devising your own 'listening tools' can provide a thinking space for the children. Using children's drawings followed by the 'children's talk' could also be a strategy used as a way of 'giving voice' allowing children to represent their feelings and explore and learn. Providing these opportunities empowers children to communicate meanings about the topics that are of meaning to them (Angelides and Michaelidou, 2009; Robert-Holmes, 2011 cited in Mukherji and Albon, 2015).

THINKING ACTIVITY

Research the Mosaic Approach. Consider the different ways in which you could use each method as a way of listening to children's voice.

Case study

Tabaseya's work centred on how a reception class teacher gained understanding of children's interests and then implemented them within a classroom setting. Throughout the research reference is made to key voice mechanisms and the implications that they have for supporting children and young people's voice. Tabaseya's research evidenced the need for practitioners to be willing and able to draw upon models and frameworks to help them give and listen to children's voice. Listening to children was a theme throughout her research, it was deemed to be imperative and essential, as was empowering and consulting children if the methods and frameworks utilised were to be effective.

The research evidenced the importance of the Mosaic Approach which was seen as being pivotal in helping elicit children's views and to help them to communicate with one another and with their teachers. Tabaseya's work emphasised the importance of effective listening cycles to help empower young children to voice their views, with teachers needing to both provide opportunities and mechanisms to capture voice (Edwards, Gandin and Foreman, 1998; Mazzei, 2007). Tabasseya makes specific reference to the use of a 'challenge box' as a mechanism for voice. Located within the classroom, the children used it to post things that they had enjoyed when playing. Children were also encouraged to make suggestions about things/games that they would like to do play. Whilst there has been criticism levelled at this as a mechanism, as it may not aid literacy development and take account of silence (Bruce, 2005, Mazzei, 2007), on this occasion, given the understanding that the teacher clearly had of her class and their needs, the mechanism worked well. The mechanism helped the teacher to foster a communicative relationship with the young children and empower them to express themselves.

Ultimately, Tabaseya's study helps to explain the complex nature of voice and the need to offer children a number of mechanisms to express their voice and the need for teachers to develop their professional skill-set to help them listen to children.

THINKING ACTIVITY

Access Development Matters and the Characteristics for Effective Learning (Early Education, 2012). After discussion with your placement mentor undertake an observation of a target child to find out where their favourite places to play are. Using aspects of the Mosaic Approach (drawings, maps, photographs, narrative accounts etc.) provide evidence for the child's learning journey that will be shared with the class teacher and parents.

Conclusion

This chapter has considered several theories and models of empowerment concerning the voice of children in the early years sector. You have been encouraged throughout to evaluate the complexities of the UNCRC; in doing so you have taken account of international, political, socio-economic, ethical and cultural implications. This chapter has given you the opportunity to develop your understanding of children's capacity and opportunity to express their voice through the analysis of case studies. Each of the case studies that are included help to enhance your understanding of voice by suggesting how specific settings are encouraging children and young people's active participation to influence policy in a range of different settings. The case studies explore the significance of voice and identify appropriate responses to key and topical issues. Analysis of the case studies should have allowed you to become more effective in responding to the needs of children and help you to ensure that they have a voice and that they are truly listened to. Ultimately, the aim of this chapter was to help you to improve your effectiveness in responding to the needs of children so you can encourage them to participate meaningfully, in doing so you will influence policy in an early years context.

Additional reading

Hart, R. (1992) *Children's participation: from tokenism to citizenship*. Florence: UNICEF International Child Development Centre.

Gilson, C. (2013) Children's rights and children's voice. In Wild, M. and Street, A. (Eds), *Themes and debates in Early Childhood*. London: Sage.

Glazzard, J. (2012). Tuning into children's voices: exploring the perceptions of primary aged children about their education in one primary school in England. *International Journal of Education*, 4 (3), 49–66.

Hallett, C. and Prout, A. (2003) Hearing the voices of children: social policy for a new century. London: Routledge.

James, A. and James, J. (2012). *Key concepts in childhood studies*. 2nd edn. London: Sage.

Useful websites

UNICEF – www.unicef.org.uk/?sisearchengine=377&siproduct=Campaign_%2A%2ABrand-Unicef-Exact.

Rights Approach in Wales – www.childcomwales.org.uk/our-work/resources/right-way-childrens-rights-approach-wales/.

Scotland – www.gov.scot/Topics/People/Young-People/gettingitright/publications/uncrc-girfec-report.

Human Rights – www.equalityhumanrights.com/en/human-rights.

Human Rights Act – www.legislation.gov.uk/ukpga/1989/42/schedule1/part/1/chapter/9.

References

Angelides, P. and Michaelidou, A. (2009) The deafening silence: discussing children's drawings for understanding and addressing marginalisation. *Journal of Early Childhood Research*, 7 (1), 27–45.

Bragg, S. (2007) 'But I listen to children anyway!'—teacher perspectives on pupil voice. *Educational Action Research*, 15 (4), 505–518.

Brooker, L. (2011) Taking children seriously: an alternative agenda for research? *Journal of Early Childhood Research*, 9 (2), 137–149.

Brownhill, S. (2014) *Empowering the children's and young people's workforce: practice based knowledge, skills and understanding*. London: Routledge.

Bruce, T. (2005) *Early childhood education*. London: Hodder and Stoughton.

Burnitt, M. and Gunter, H. (2013) Primary school councils: organizations, composition and head teacher perceptions and values. *Management in Education*, 27 (2), 56–62.

Children Act (1989) *C.41*. [online]. Available at: www.legislation.gov.uk/ukpga/1989/41/contents [accessed 4 March 2018].

Children Act (2004) *C31*. [online]. Available at: www.legislation.gov.uk/ukpga/2004/31/contents [accessed 4th March 2018].

Clark, A. and Moss, P. (2001) *Listening to young children: the Mosaic Approach*. London: National Children's Bureau for the Joseph Rowntree Foundation.

Clark, A. and Moss, P. (2011) *Listening to young children: the Mosaic Approach*. 2nd edn. London: National Children's Bureau for the Joseph Rowntree Foundation.

Covell, K. R. and McNeil, J.K. (2010) Implementing children's human rights education in schools. *Improving Schools*, 13 (2), 117–132.

Cox, S. and Robinson-Pant, A. (2005) Challenging perceptions of school counsels in primary schools. *Education 3–13*, 33 (2), 14–19.

Czerniawsli, G. and Kidd, W. (2011). *The student voice handbook: bridging the academic/practitioner divide*. UK: Emerald Publishing Ltd.

Davie, R., Upton, G. and Varma, V. (Eds) (1996) *The voice of the child. A Handbook for Professionals*. London: Falmer Press.

Davies, L., Williams, C., Yamashita, H. and Ko Man-Hing, A. (2006) *Inspiring schools, impact and outcomes: taking up the challenge of pupil participation*. London: Carnegie Young People Initiative and Esmee Fairbairn Foundation.

Department for Children Schools and Families (2007).*The children's plan: building brighter futures*. [online]. Available at: www.gov.uk/government/publications/the-childrens-plan [accessed 4 March 2018].

Department for Children Schools and Families (2008) *Children's plan one year on*. [online]. Available at: www.gov.uk/government/publications/the-childrens-plan [accessed 4 March 2018].

Department for Education (2014) *Listening to and involving children and young people*. London: Crown copyright.

Department for Education and Skills (2003) *Every child matters*. London: Department for Education and Skills.

Donaldson, J. (2000). *Monkey puzzle*. London: MacMillan Children's Books.

Dubiel, J. (2016) *Effective assessment in the early years*. London: Sage.

Early Education (2012) *Development matters in the early years foundation stage* (EYFS). London: Early Education.

Edwards, C., Gandin, L. and Foreman, G. (1998) *The hundred languages of children: the Reggio Emilia approach to early childhood education*. 2nd edn. New Jersey: Ablex Public Corporation.

Graf, M. (2011) *Including and supporting learners of English as an additional language*. New York: Continuum International Publishing Group.

Green, S. and Hill, M. (2005) *Researching children's experience: methods and methodological issues*. In Greene, S. and Hogan, D. (Eds), *Researching children's experience: approaches and methods*. London: Sage.

Hart, R. (1992) *Children's Participation: From Tokenism to Citizenship*. Florence: UNICEF International Child Development Centre.

James, A. and Prout, A. (Eds) (1990) *Constructing and reconstructing childhood: contemporary issues in the sociological study of childhood*. Cambridge: Polity Press.

Kilvington, J and Wood, A. (2016) *Gender, sex and Children's play*. London: Bloomsbury Publishing Plc.

Lansdown, G. (1994) Children's rights. In Mayall, B. (Ed.) *Children's childhoods: observed and experienced* (pp. 33–44). London: Falmer Press.

Lundy, L. (2007) Voice is not enough: conceptualising Article 12 of the United Nations Convention on the Rights of the Child. *British Educational Research Journal*, 33 (6), 927–942.

Mazzei, L. (2007) Towards a problematic of silence in action research. *Educational Action Research*, 15 (4), 631–642.

Moosa-Mitha, M. (2005). A difference-centred alternative to theorization of children's citizenship rights. *Citizenship Studies*, 9 (4), 369–388.

Mukherji., P. and Albon, A. (2015) *Research methods in early childhood: an introductory guide*. 2nd edn. London: Sage.

Office of the United Nations High Commissioner for Human Rights (1989) *Convention on the Rights of the Child*. Geneva: The Office of the United Nations High Commissioner for Human Rights.

O'Quigley, A. (2000) *Listening to children's views: the findings and recommendations of recent research*. Joseph Rowntree Foundation. York: YPS.

Qvortrup J. (1994) Introduction. In Qvortrup J., Bardy M., Sgritta G. and Wintersberger H. (Eds), *Childhood Matters. Social Theory, Practice and Politics* (pp. 1–23). Aldershot: Avebury.

Robert-Holmes, G. (2011) *Doing your early years research project: a step-by-step guide*. 2nd edn. London: Sage.

Robinson, C. and Taylor, C. (2013) Student voice as a contested practice: power and participation in two student voice projects. *Improving schools*, 16 (1), 32–46.

Roche, J. (1999) Children and divorce: a private affair? In Shelley Day-Sclater, S. and Piper, C. (Eds), *Undercurrents of divorce*. Aldershot: Ashgate Publishing Ltd.

Rudduck, J. and Flutter, J. (2000) Pupil participation and pupil perspective: carving a new order of experience. *Cambridge Journal of Education*, 30 (1), 75–89.

Sebba, J. and Robinson, C. (2010) *Evaluation of UNICEF UK's Rights Respecting Schools Award*. [online]. Available at: https://rrscanada.files.wordpress.com/2013/05/rrsa-uk-evaluation [accessed 14 March 2018].

Servos, J., Dewar, B., Bosacki, S. and Coplan, R. (2017) Canadian early childhood educators' perceptions of role-play and cultural identity. *Journal of Early Childhood Research*, 14 (3), 324–332.

Sorin, R. (2003) Research with children: a rich glimpse into the world of childhood. *Australian Journal of Early Childhood*, 28 (1), 31–35.

Spyrou, S. (2016) Researching children's silences: exploring the fullness of voice in childhood research. *Childhood*, 23 (1), 7–21.

Tangen, D. and Spooner-Lane, R. (2008) Avoiding the deficit model of teaching: students who have EAL and learning difficulties. *Australian Journal of Learning Difficulties*, 13 (2), 63–71.

United Nations (1989) *United Nations Convention on the Rights of the Child* (UNCRC). Geneva: United Nations.

Westcott, H. and Littleton, K. (2005) Exploring meaning through interviews with children. In Greene, S. and Hogan, D. (Eds), *Researching children's experience: approaches and methods* (pp. 141–157). London, UK: Sage Publications Ltd.

Whitty, G. and Wisby, E. (2007) Whose voice? An exploration of the current policy interest in pupil involvement in school decision-making. *International Studies in Sociology of Education*, 17 (3), 303–319.

Woodhead, M. and Faulkner, D. (2008) Subjects, objects or participants? Dilemmas of psychological research with children. In P. Christensen and A. James (Eds), *Research with children: perspectives and practices*. 2nd edn. Abingdon: Routledge.

Chapter 5

Becoming an advanced practitioner

Amanda Crow and Wayne Bailey

CHAPTER AIMS

By the end of this chapter you will:

- have identified the knowledge skills and attributes necessary for an advanced practitioner working in early years
- have an understanding of the concept of mentoring and what this means for an early years practitioner
- understand why professional relationships matter and the importance of developing a successful partnership with your mentor
- have identified the traits that will help you to succeed as a graduate practitioner.

Introduction

This chapter will focus on your role as an advanced practitioner in early years and will recognise that work-based learning is an integral part of the undergraduate journey for early years practitioners. Becoming competent in practice requires the student to draw upon their knowledge, skills and attributes when working with their immediate teams and also with a range of outside agencies. It is also important that practitioners are self-reflective and able to be self-critical. The role of the placement mentor and the importance of developing a respectful relationship are essential, as is working with other team members. Consequently, this chapter encourages you to explore your role as educator, carer and colleague within an early years context.

You will evaluate and consider the complexities of different approaches to working in partnership, helping and supporting others whilst being supported to develop your own professional self. This will enable you to work more effectively with your mentor. Developing your pedagogical approach will also be examined from the perspective that as you gain in confidence you will be developing leadership traits that will support your developing practice. We will explore pedagogical leadership and how theory influences your practice, examining your personal attitudes to children, parents and colleagues. Finally, the chapter will explore how these attitudes and attributes can equip you with the tools to forge ahead with your career in early years.

Being an advanced practitioner: what does this mean in practice?

Once you have gained confidence in your practice and embarked on your second and subsequent years of study, developing and refining your skills will enable you to become a competent advanced practitioner. This will require you to draw on knowledge and attributes gained from both academic work and your placement practice. Understanding the importance of developing successful professional relationships with fellow practitioners, parents and a range of outside agencies is therefore essential, as is working closely and under the guidance of an experienced mentor.

Work-based learning is an important aspect of your developing professionalism and should have equal status to your academic learning. Work-based learning is increasingly seen as offering opportunities to strengthen your approach to practice (Stobbs and Musgrave, 2017). It is an essential opportunity to develop your own approach to early years pedagogy, as learning from experience and broadening your knowledge and skills will enable you to draw on and strengthen your professional characteristics. As an emerging advanced practitioner, you will have successfully completed your foundation year, including a positive placement experience in one or more early years settings. Being advanced now means taking a lead, using your initiative, being resourceful and taking responsibility. As an advanced practitioner you will need to develop the ability to be self-critical as you reflect more deeply on your practice.

Theory to practice

Often, you will hear your tutors talk about applying theory to practice, or there will be comments on your assessed work that suggests that you need to apply theory to practice. This is a term used to explain how your developing theoretical understanding of how children learn and develop is used to inform your practical work with children. Theoretical frameworks help you to question yourself and others, to assess and interact with children, their families and the environment.

THINKING ACTIVITY

1   In taught sessions you will have discussed a range of child development theorists and pioneers and how their beliefs have influenced our knowledge of the developing child. Do you write about these influencers in your written work?
2   Think back to the comments you have received so far on your assessed work – have you had feedback that asks you to provide evidence of your understanding of development theories?
3   One of the comments that occurs regularly for students is to read more widely about child development – has this been the case for you?

Child development involves a complex pattern of change (Doherty and Hughes, 2013), therefore, early years practitioners need to be aware of and examine the changes that occur as the child grows and develops. There are a large number of books and journal articles readily available which discuss theoretical approaches to child development; this chapter does not intend to compete with them. What it suggests is the importance of how you reflect with others, fellow students, tutors and colleagues in early years settings to critically evaluate how theory impacts on your understanding of children and childhood.

The EYFS offers four overarching principles to shape and guide practice; these principles help us to understand our roles and the way we interact, assess and celebrate the holistic development of children:

- Every child is a unique child, who is constantly learning and can be resilient, capable, confident and self-assured.
- Children learn to be strong and independent through positive relationships.
- Children learn and develop well in enabling environments, in which their experiences respond to their individual needs and there is a strong partnership between practitioners and parents and/or carers.
- Children develop and learn in different ways and at different rates. The framework principles acknowledge that all children are unique and have individual needs.

(DfE, 2017, p. 6)

THINKING ACTIVITY

The EYFS asks us to consider the unique child, who is constantly learning. What evidence do you see of this in practice?

Spend some time thinking about the practitioners you see and how they interact with the children, can you identify how they help them to be confident and self-assured?

What does the environment look like, does it enable children to be independent and resilient?

How is partnership with parents and/or carers encouraged, do practitioners and parents share the child's day, in what ways is this evidenced?

Using critical reflection

In early years practice the act of reflective practice provides opportunities to evaluate your work with children, their families and colleagues (Dyer and Firth, 2018). Reflection is about analysis (Brock, 2015) and practitioners can use reflection to problem solve and engage in ideas that will improve practice. It should be acknowledged, however, that reflection is an emotional business; it can be enlightening but also challenging. Reflective practice can therefore enable you to work more effectively and to use your developing knowledge from your university studies to help you understand the what, how and why of children's behaviour.

Using reflective practice to develop expertise with your mentor will encourage you to be self-aware and self-critical. These traits, when encouraged, can offer an approach to developing deeper professional learning (National College for Teaching and

Leadership (NCTL), 2013). Learning through professional conversations is further reinforced by Brock (2015, p. 28) who explains that reflection with others can deepen theoretical understanding and promote professionalism. Ideally you will have regular opportunities through mentor meetings, where you have the space to examine your actions, to think together, to question and be challenged, as this will reinforce deeper learning and offer you the opportunity to engage in sustained shared thinking (Brock, 2015, p. 22). Additionally, deeper learning can be reinforced through context specific experiences, reinforcing the benefit of learning together, sharing experiences and reflecting on child development. Key to your professional development and learning would appear to be a successful relationship with your mentor (Appleby, 2010).

Working collaboratively with your mentor, reflecting on your learning together will increase your opportunity to think and learn deeply. This process can be explained through reflexivity, reflecting on situations and how you have achieved them. Brock (2015) describes reflexivity as being able to observe, appraise and tease out actions, to examine and develop by engaging in deep critical questioning. Furthermore, the reflexive practitioner is not only adept at self-reflection but also considers the wider implications on practice of political and cultural influences (Hayes, 2017), reinforcing the importance of combining theory to practice.

Reflection is more than just thinking and talking through situations in order to develop, it involves critically analysing practice through dialogue and discussion (Brock, 2015). The reflective process should also involve questioning your own values, morals and beliefs, analysing how and why you do something and having the ability to see yourself through the eyes of others. The work of Dewey, a key pioneer in reflective thinking, can be used as an approach, suggests Brock (2015). Using Dewey's philosophy of reflecting on experience can encourage you to problem solve with your mentor. Likewise combining the work of Schön (1976) and the process of reflecting 'in and on' action engages you to examine what you naturally do in practice, together with considering how 'on' reflection you further improve and develop. This process when undertaken with your mentor can, as Brock explains, enable you to use theory to reflect on your practice, deepen your understanding of why you act the way you do and offers possibilities to analyse your decision making and plan ahead (Brock, 2015, p. 12).

THINKING ACTIVITY

Think about a professional conversation you have had with your mentor during an arranged meeting. How did the discussion start? Who took the lead in the conversation? Did you reflect on a particular experience or more generally on your everyday practice? Were you aware of following a particular model or theory?

Identify goals and planning your professional learning

Alongside planning for the children, it is good practice to engage in planning for your own development. This can be done using a number of methods that essentially involve you planning, evaluating and reflecting on your experiences. Just as planning for children's learning involves observation and assessment, so does planning for your own learning and developing a greater understanding of your own actions.

Dyer and Firth (2018) suggest confidence is required when moving from novice to experienced practitioner. This developing confidence can lead you to experiment and be creative when identifying your personal learning needs. Using contracts to identify your own goals and learning outcomes is one such method that can help you to recognise, manage and assess both the learning intentions of your written work, alongside setting goals for your professional development. Although it may seem a formal approach, a contract is a way of agreeing both your own priorities for learning and commitment to the setting. Table 5.1 is an example of a contract currently used to support Year 2 undergraduate students.

ACTIVITY

Using the contract example below, identify 3 learning outcomes that you would like to achieve in placement and complete the columns in the table using the headings to guide you.

Table 5.1 Example of a contract currently used to support Year 2 undergraduate students

Student name:		Date:		Contract number:
Setting:		Mentor:		
Learning outcome	Learning resources/ strategies	Evidence of achievement	Deadline	Mentor signature
Identify 2 or 3 things you will learn by the end of the contract	List any actions needed to help you learn for example help from others or opportunities to carry out tasks	Include evidence you use to prove you have learned something new	Set yourself a realistic timescale, you may need to work on a contract over a number of weeks in order to achieve your outcomes	Each outcome signed to confirm it is achieved

Share your ideas with your mentor, was this a helpful way to identify and negotiate your learning needs?

The importance of mentoring in early years

To develop as an advanced practitioner requires a number of professional working relationships. Mentors play a vital role in supporting learning and helping students to manage their work on a day-to-day basis, they also provide an essential link between your placement and the academic aspects of your early years course. The opportunity to plan and set goals with your mentor has many benefits, in particular the ability to integrate your university and practical learning to enhance your skill set, and develop your professional status as an advanced practitioner.

Mentoring can be described as a one-to-one relationship that takes place between an experienced and less experienced person with the purpose of learning, or developing specific competencies. It has been described as a form of planned helping which supports less-experienced individuals in their development (Crisp and Cruz, 2009; Terrion and Leonard, 2007; Gannon and Maher, 2012). Successful mentoring is a process that leads to a change in thinking that empowers individuals to grow, to develop knowledge and understanding about strategies that will help to improve their practice (Bailey and Schoch, 2011; Brockbank and McGill, 2012; Bailey et al., 2015; Aderibigbe, Colucci-Gray and Gray, 2016; Thompson 2016).

THINKING ACTIVITY

Before you meet with your placement mentor for the first time, think about what mentoring is and what it means to you. Find a definition of mentoring that resonates; be ready to discuss it with your mentor at your first meeting.

Key features of effective mentoring in early years

McMahon, Dyer and Baker (2016) suggest that effective mentoring has a number of features, but that the setting of goals, achievement criteria and timescales are key, if a successful relationship between mentor and mentee is to be fostered, nurtured and maintained. The work of the mentor and the mentee has to be complimentary, and whilst there needs to be action from both parties, professional development should be the focus.

The right mixture of support and challenge is needed if both you and your mentor are to get the most out of the relationship. Clearly, agreeing the 'right blend' of the support/challenge 'cocktail' is not an exact science, and it is something that may change as you become more experienced, or if you come up against a particular challenge that is new. What is clear is that any challenge agreed between you and your mentor, with your development in mind, needs to be 'scaffolded' with the right amount of support. This needs to take place within an atmosphere that is conducive to your development, and is nurtured by empathy, rapport and trust (Spooner-Lane 2017). As a first year student it is likely that your relationships with your tutors and mentors were highly supportive and that this gave you the confidence to develop and to grow. As you begin your journey to become an advanced practitioner, you can expect to be offered more challenge from your mentor. Do not worry about this, your mentor will be mindful of your particular needs and will work with you to get the right mix of challenge/support that is appropriate for you. When thinking about the support/challenge 'cocktail' that is highlighted above, Daloz's (1986) model of mentoring relations is worth considering (Figure 5.1).

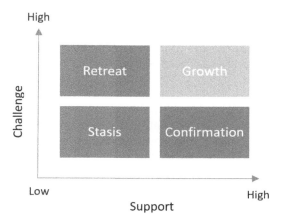

Figure 5.1 Daloz's model of mentoring relations.
Adapted from Daloz (1986, p. 208).

Throughout your relationship with your mentor, if the amount of support and challenge you are offered is low, then little development will take place (stasis). Whereas, if your mentor challenges you too much, without an appropriate amount of support, then you are likely to 'retreat' and could even leave your placement. Equally unproductive is the relationship that offers too much support with little or no challenge. If you have this type of relationship with your placement mentor, then once more there is likely to be little sustained development. If you are to become an advanced practitioner, who develops and 'grows' throughout your career, then it is vitally important that you work with your mentor to ensure that you are offered the right amount of support and challenge. This can be a particularly delicate balance that requires discussion with your mentor (Daloz, 1986).

Case study

Jane is an experienced early years practitioner and has worked at a setting for three years, she is mentor to Becky who is on placement at the nursery. Jane takes her role as a mentor very seriously and wants to help Becky as much as she can. She has spent much of the last two months supporting Becky and is very reluctant to challenge her because this makes Becky uncomfortable. Jane has become increasingly worried that Becky has become over-reliant on her and that she is not developing as quickly as she expected her to. Becky is reluctant to try anything new and asks for help all of the time and expects too much of Jane.

1 Think about Jane and Becky's relationship.
2 What could Jane do to help get the relationship back on track?

In order to ensure that an atmosphere is created that is conducive to developing as an advanced practitioner, Bailey et al. (2015) suggest that a good mentor should:

- be friendly, approachable and professional in order to help build rapport
- listen actively and question appropriately
- encourage reflection.

Championing an approach to mentoring that is underpinned by reflection requires a positive mentor/mentee working relationship. Encouragement from your mentor is paramount, as is a friendly and appropriate manner, if you are to develop an open and productive relationship. During your early meetings with your mentor, take the opportunity to devise a mentoring contract that makes it explicit what each party can expect from the other throughout their relationship. You could adapt the contract discussed earlier in this chapter, see the example in Table 5.1. Remember, the mentoring contract is not set in stone. It is something that should be reviewed periodically, or when what is needed from the relationship changes. However, in the first instance, when writing a mentoring contract, you might want to think about the following:

- How long the relationship will last?
- How often will you meet and for how long?
- What is expected of both the mentor and mentee in between meetings?
- What are the roles of the mentor and mentee during the relationship?
- What aspects of the relationship are confidential and which are not?

Your mentor needs to listen actively and should ask probing, insightful questions that allow them to get to the nub of any issues that are impacting on your development whilst on placement. Brewer (2016) refers to the need to have a *'mentoring attitude'* which requires your mentor to value their own learning as part of their relationship with you, if they are to help you develop. This requires an open mind, trust, positivity, encouragement, respectfulness and appropriate challenge, particularly if rapport is to be built. Your mentor should also evidence active listening by summarising and paraphrasing during your meetings. This, in conjunction with using probing, open questions, can help to ensure that you explore issues fully (Wallace and Gravells, 2007) and reflect appropriately about development needs, so you can put in place an action plan that enables you to move forward. Your professional development needs should be the focus of your relationship with your mentor.

As touched upon, what you require from your mentor will change over time. Have the confidence to shape your relationship with your mentor, this is an important element of your development as an advanced practitioner. Remember mentoring should not be a 'one size fits all' approach, take the initiative, organise meetings, summarise what has been discussed and action plan (Crow and McMahon, 2018). Understanding what mentoring is, what a professional mentor should do, the traits of a good mentee, and what makes a healthy and productive relationship before you start your placement will help you to get the most out of the relationship, and to develop as an advanced practitioner.

Case study

Danielle is having an excellent experience with her mentor (Brooke) on placement. Brooke has helped her to identify a number of things that should enable her to develop as an advanced practitioner. Danielle was pleasantly surprised that Brooke knew things about her course and that she was willing to offer advice and guidance. Danielle meets with Brooke weekly. However, if there are times when it is difficult due to staffing or the time of day, Danielle knows that she can e-mail Brooke and that they will meet later that week.

At their first meeting, Brooke and Danielle develop a contract together. Whilst Brooke made it clear what was expected from Danielle, she also explained what Danielle could expect from her in return. This reassured Danielle. The starting point of the relationship was the nursery's student policy introduced at Danielle's induction. Throughout the induction Brooke discussed all the information that Danielle needed to feel comfortable with whilst on placement.

Brooke is friendly and approachable and although, as part of the contracting process, it was agreed that they would meet weekly, Danielle feels confident about approaching Brooke if an issue arises that she is anxious about. Brooke is always professional in her approach, yet friendly, which has enabled the pair to build a strong rapport. Danielle has noticed that Brooke actively listens whenever they meet and that she makes a point of summarising and paraphrasing aspects of the conversation that has taken place. This gives Danielle confidence. Reflection is always a key element of their meetings with Danielle being encouraged to think about what is, and is not, going well. Brooke asks open question that encourage Danielle to reflect on her weekly experiences and each session finishes with Danielle taking the lead on devising a plan of action for the coming week. Although Brooke has challenged Danielle more as the weeks have gone by, Danielle is really positive about the experience and feels like she is developing as an advanced practitioner.

1   Reflect on the approaches of both Brooke and Danielle.
2   What is it that they are doing that is enabling them to foster a positive mentor/mentee relationship?
3   Think about the features of effective mentoring.
4   What can you do to make sure that you get the most out your relationship with your work-based mentor?

The role of coaching within the mentoring relationship

There are subtle differences between mentoring and coaching. For instance, there has been much debate and discussion about the differing focus of mentoring and coaching, about the length of the relationship, whether skills or capabilities are to be developed and discussion about who drives the relationship itself. Interestingly, Clutterbuck (2014) suggests that mentoring and coaching are not mutually exclusive but in fact complimentary. When you worked with your mentor during the first year of your course, there will have been times when you were involved in coaching conversations as part of an overall mentoring strategy. You will likely recollect times that you undertook a task on placement, after agreeing it with your mentor, which you reviewed after the event and for which you were given constructive feedback. Your mentor may have even shown you what to do beforehand, and given you the opportunity to observe and subsequently asked questions about what they saw and what took place. This approach is what Clutterbuck would call 'show and tell' coaching (2014).

As you become an advanced practitioner, it is very likely that your mentor will continue to use coaching as part of an overall mentoring strategy. However, you will probably notice a different approach being taken to coaching as you gain experience, both on the course and within your placement setting. As a student who is developing as an advanced practitioner, you may notice subtle differences in the coaching that takes place, which Clutterbuck calls suggestive/simulative coaching (Clutterbuck, 2014). As you work with your mentor, he or she is much more likely to expect feedback to be provided by you rather than by them. You will be expected to think about things yourself and as a result of conversation with your mentor self-analyse, reflect and action plan for the future. You will be expected to take more of a lead in this process.

What if the relationship is not working?

Crow and McMahon (2018) point out that whilst relationships between a mentor and mentee are on the whole fruitful and positive, on occasion, relationships can breakdown. If you find yourself in a relationship that is not working, it is important that you deal with the issue(s) professionally. Hopefully you will feel confident enough to discuss any problems with your mentor directly. However, if this is not possible, you need to bring it to the attention of your course tutor. If the relationship becomes untenable, as a last resort, the decision to move placement could be taken. Any such action would be approached sensitively and respectfully.

THINKING ACTIVITY

Identify the barriers to effective mentoring as presented in Crow and McMahon (2018) and identify the conditions which will support effective mentoring.

Whilst barriers to effective mentoring exist, as highlighted above, there are a number of features to mentoring which, if understood and adhered to, can heighten the chances of you having a positive relationship with your work-based mentor.

Case study

Lauren is a second year student; she has been on placement for one month and her relationship with Tracy, her placement mentor, has not developed in the manner that she had hoped. Lauren is a conscientious student who works hard, and had prepared prior to her first mentor meeting because she wanted to get the most out of her relationship with Tracy. Unfortunately, Lauren does not feel at all supported in her placement. Tracy shows little interest in Lauren's development and never seems to have time to work with her. On the few occasions that Lauren has had the opportunity to work with her mentor, Tracy decides what is and is not discussed. Tracy makes Lauren feel that her issues are of little consequence and are not worth discussing. Tracy spends most of the meeting talking at Lauren and not listening to her; she is very serious and there is very little rapport between Lauren and her mentor.

Clearly this relationship is not working for Lauren. What would you suggest she could do to get the relationship back on track?

Relationships matter

Working closely with your mentor during your training will offer you many opportunities to grow and develop as a practitioner; therefore, a trusting relationship built on respect is something to aim for. Hayes (2016) discusses professionalism in early practice in relation to balancing a number of responsibilities. As you gain experience you will become increasingly aware of the complex mix of legal and political requirements that influence early years practice; this will usually be through Acts of Parliament, government policy and local procedural interpretations at local authority and setting level. Alongside being accountable for implementing legislation you will also be influenced by your own personal values and this will influence your moral and ethical beliefs (Hayes, 2016).

The EYFS 3.20 p 21 states:

> The quality of provision depends on all practitioners having appropriate qualifications, training, skills and knowledge and a clear understanding of roles and responsibilities.
>
> (DfE, 2017)

Your mentor will ideally be an experienced/senior member of staff and someone you will be able to question and engage in critical discussion; this process will enable you to build on and develop professional qualities in a safe respectful environment. According to Hayes (2016) professionalism requires the practitioner to be trustworthy, therefore, respect and confidentiality are of equal importance when establishing a successful mentor/mentee relationship. Education and early years practice is ever changing and pressure to offer quality services that make a positive difference to children's learning and development is high on the political agenda (Ofsted, 2013).

Professional learning, and developing people, matters more than ever as practitioners are accountable for the quality of care and education of society's youngest children (NCTL, 2013).

The relationship with your mentor will be developmental and, metaphorically speaking, mentoring can be viewed as a journey (Mullen, 2012). The concept of a journey suggests both mentor and mentee engage in a journey of learning which is reciprocal and mutually beneficial to each other and the children and families they support. Mullen (2012) describes collaborative mentoring theory as a proactive force that unites individuals and groups. This theory is a helpful interpretation of mentoring in the early years as, often, the relationship with your mentor is not exclusive, and depending on the size and structure of your setting, you may work with small or large teams of practitioners.

This may mean that you find yourself in a dynamic collaborative relationship and other team members are also involved in your mentoring journey.

Case study

Jenny is on placement in a large day-care setting, and her mentor Fiona, is the room leader of a pre-school room for children aged 3–4 years. Although Jenny has regular meetings with Fiona, there are also times when Jenny is working alongside a number of different practitioners and her mentor is not available. Jenny is aware that she is a team member in the pre-school room and has developed relationships with her fellow practitioners. She has made agreements with Fiona and her university that she will liaise with all staff, and that they will influence and help her to develop practice. There is also a speech and language therapist that attends the setting to support two children. Seeing this as an opportunity to develop further, Jenny has asked her mentor if she can gain experience of working with the speech therapist.

1   Can you think of any challenges and opportunities that Jenny might face when working with a range of different practitioners?
2   What skills will Jenny be able to develop by working with a number of different practitioners?
3   Communication with her mentor will be crucial; how will Jenny be able to maintain professional relationships with each of her colleagues and her mentor?

Communities of practice

Working with the wider professional children's workforce will offer you the opportunity to understand the many different roles involved in supporting children and families. The EYFS requires practitioners to link with and help families to access, relevant services (DfE, 2017). As early years practitioners this means you will be required to work with parents and/or carers and a number of agencies that are also responsible for the health and welfare of young children. One of the theories that can be applied to your learning with others in placement is 'Communities of Practice' (Stobbs and

Musgrave, 2017, p. 136). Building on Lave and Wenger's (1991) theory, your involvement in a variety of communities including internal and external colleagues, parents/carers can be seen as an important vehicle for learning. Lave and Wenger describe this as a process of social learning. Taking advantage of learning through a variety of social networks reinforces your shared purpose and goals of supporting children's learning and development.

Moving forward and becoming employable

Developing your pedagogical role with children and their families involves recognising your own abilities and using them to learn with, and to influence, others. As you come to the end of your early years degree you will have gained a wealth of experience to take forward after graduation. The graduate practitioner recognises their own skills, knowledge and attributes and how these will continue to influence practice. Being self-aware will be essential as you consolidate your learning and plan for your next steps. Whilst working with others you will have started to gain transferable skills, through team working and partnerships, and although leadership skills may not be something you readily acknowledge, nevertheless, they will have been gained. Personalising and leading your own learning with your mentor, planning for children's learning and encouraging the cooperation of colleagues and parents, are possible examples.

McMahon (2017) states that pedagogical leadership involves the practitioner taking a holistic approach to their work, acknowledging the importance of child development, teaching and learning influenced by personal values and beliefs. This view reinforces the belief that all practitioners have the potential to demonstrate pedagogical leadership, through sharing responsibilities and engaging in partnership (Nutbrown, 2012). Leadership in early years settings develops through relationships (Hallet, 2013), working closely with your mentor and taking every advantage from your placement setting. This will prepare you for the next stage of your pedagogical journey.

ACTIVITY

Write a short reflective account describing and analysing your learning through your placement experience. Identify any leadership skills you have developed during your time at the placement. How do these skills fit with your understanding of pedagogical leadership explored in this chapter? Now discuss your reflection with your mentor, be proactive, encourage your mentor to challenge you by asking questions.

Conclusion

This chapter has explored your developing role as an advanced practitioner, acknowledging the benefits of a successful mentor/mentee relationship and how this will enhance your pedagogical learning. Work-based learning is an important aspect of your university studies, and the experiences gained in placement will enhance your development and enable you to understand how theory and policy inform your practice. Engaging in professional conversations can lead to deeper learning and critical reflection (Brock, 2015), and these professional relationships are essential for your future employment.

References

Aderibigbe, S., Colucci-Gray, L. and Gray, D. (2016) Conceptions and expectations of mentoring relationships in a teacher education reform context, mentoring and tutoring. *Partnership in Learning*, 24 (1), 8–29.

Appleby, K. (2010) Reflective thinking: reflective practice. In Reed, M. and Canning, N. *Reflective practice in the early years*. 1st. edn. London: Sage.

Bailey, W. and Schoch, J. (2011) subject specialist mentors in the lifelong learning sector: the subject specialist mentor model; is it working? *Teaching in Lifelong Learning*, 3 (1), 4–15.

Bailey, W., Blamires, Ch., Dixon, L., Iredale, A., Robinson, D. and Schoch, J. (2015) Coaching and mentoring. In *Teaching in lifelong learning: a guide to theory and practice*. Milton Keynes: Open University Press.

Brewer, A. (2016) Mentoring from a positive psychology perspective. Learning for mentors and mentees. Switzerland: Springer International Publishing.

Brock, A. (2015) The early years reflective practice handbook. London: Routledge.

Brockbank, A. and McGill, I. (2012) Facilitating reflective learning: coaching, mentoring and supervision. 2nd edn. London: Kogan Page.

Clutterbuck, D. (2014) *Everyone needs a mentor*. 5th edn. London: Chartered Institute of Personnel and Development.

Crisp, G. and Cruz, I. (2009). Mentoring college students: a critical review of the literature between 1990 and 2007. *Research in Higher Education*, 50 (6), 525–545. http://dx.doi.org/10.1007/s11162-009-9130-2.

Crow, A. and McMahon, S. (2018) Working in partnership with placement. In McMahon, S. and Dyer, M. *Work-based practice in the early years: a guide for students*. London: Routledge.

Daloz, L. (1986). Effective teaching and mentoring: realizing the transformational power of adult learning experiences. San Francisco: Jossey-Bass.

Department for Education (DfE) (2017) Statutory framework for the early years foundation stage: setting the standards for learning, development and care for children from birth to five. London: Crown Copyright.

Doherty, J. and Hughes, M. (2013) *Child development: theory and practice 0–11*. 2nd edn. Harlow: Pearson.

Dyer, M. and Firth, N. (2018) Being a reflective practitioner. In McMahon, S. and Dyer, M. *Work-based practice in the early years*. Oxon: Routledge.

Gannon, J.M. and Maher, A. (2012) Developing tomorrow's talent: the case of an undergraduate mentoring programme. *Education + Training*, 54 (6), 440–455.

Hallet, E. (2013) 'We all share a common vision and passion': early years professionals reflect upon their leadership of practice role. *Journal of Early Childhood Research,* 11 (3), 312–325.

Hayes, C. (2016) Legal and professional responsibilities. In Trodd, L. The early years handbook for students and practitioners: an essential guide for the foundation degree and levels 4 and 5. London: Routledge.

Hayes, C. (2017) The nature of reflective practice. In Hayes, C., Daly, J., Duncan, M., Gill, R. and Whitehouse, A. *developing as a reflective early years professional*. 2nd edn. St Albans: Critical Publishing.

Lave, J. and Wenger, E. (1991) *Situated learning: legitimate peripheral participation.* Cambridge: Cambridge University Press.

McMahon, S., Dyer, M. and Baker, C. (2016) Mentoring, coaching and supervision. In *The early years handbook for students and practitioners* (pp. 433–447). London, UK Routledge.

McMahon, S. (2017) Leadership in ECEC. In McMahon, S. and Dyer, M. *Work-based practice in the early years.* Oxon: Routledge.

Mullen, C.A. (2012) Mentoring: an overview. In Fletcher, S. and Mullen, C.A. *The SAGE handbook of mentoring and coaching in education.* 1st edn. London: SAGE.

National College for Teaching and Leadership (2013) *Empowering others: coaching and mentoring.* Thinkpiece. Crown copyright.

Nutbrown, C. (2012) Foundations for quality: the Independent Review of early Education and Childcare Qualifications: Final Report. London: Department for Education.

Ofsted (2013) Getting it right first time. Achieving and maintaining high quality early years provision, reference 130117. Manchester: Ofsted.

Schön, D. (1976) The reflective practitioner: how professionals think in action. Aldershot: Arena.

Spooner-Lane, R. (2017) Mentoring beginning teachers in primary schools: research review. *Professional Development in Education,* 43 (2), 253–273.

Stobbs, N. and Musgrave, J. (2017) Learning in the workplace. In Musgrave, J., Savin-Baden, M. and Stobbs, N. *Studying for your early years degree. Skills and knowledge for becoming an effective practitioner.* St Albans: Critical Publishing.

Terrion, J. and Leonard, D. (2007) A taxonomy of the characteristics of student peer mentors in higher education: findings from a literature review. *Mentoring & Tutoring: Partnership in Learning,* 15 (2), 149–164. doi:10.1080/13611260601086311.

Thompson, C. (2016) The magic of mentoring, a democratic approach to mentoring trainee teachers in post-compulsory education. *Research in Post-Compulsory Education,* 21 (3), 246–259.

Wallace, S. and Gravells, J. (2007) *Mentoring in further education.* Exeter: Learning Matters.

Chapter 6

Safeguarding in practice

Amanda Crow and Lindsey Watson

CHAPTER AIMS

By the end of this chapter you will have:

- an understanding of safeguarding and promoting the welfare of young people through the eyes of a more experienced practitioner
- explored the concept of early intervention and partnership in early years practice
- reflected on a number of contemporary issues and their impact on early child development.

Introduction

This chapter will explore safeguarding policy and practices with a particular emphasis on the developing role of the advanced practitioner in early years. Protecting children from harm is an integral element of your early years practice; this chapter will reinforce the importance of legislation as you gain in confidence and experience. How this knowledge influences and informs your practice will be explored alongside the responsibilities and duties expected of practitioners who are gaining in expertise.

Keeping the child at the centre of practice is essential but has the potential to be lost, as is often reported in serious case reviews. These challenges will be explored alongside working with families and the wider children's workforce. Finally, the importance of reflective practice through supportive supervision, both peer and management, will be offered as a way to develop a holistic approach to practice that focuses on solutions rather than problems.

Safeguarding and the role of the advanced practitioner

Early years settings have a responsibility to ensure children are protected and ensure their welfare needs are at the heart of practice. Practitioners, therefore, must be sure that the environment is safe and that measures are taken to keep children safe and well (DfE, 2017 p. 16). Student practitioners completing early years and early childhood degrees often start their studies with a variety of experiences. This chapter acknowledges that you will bring to your practice, experiences that have shaped your knowledge about safeguarding. You may be starting your student life as a novice with little or no previous experience with young children, be an accomplished student who has undertaken a level 2 or 3 in childcare or an employed experienced practitioner; whatever your experience, being confident and knowing what to do when a concern arises is essential.

Working Together to Safeguard Children, published in 2015 and updated in 2017, is the overarching document that guides local authorities and children's services in their statutory duties. All children and young people have a right to be safeguarded and protected from harm (HM Government, 2015a). The law relating to safeguarding children is constantly being revised and updated; therefore, keeping in touch with changes in legislation must be an integral aspect of your safeguarding training, both in the setting and throughout your academic studies.

The development of current legislation

The current Working Together to Safeguard Children document has itself been through a number of developments and changes since its initial publication. The guidance, first published in 1988, coincided with a public inquiry that reported the findings of an investigation into child sexual abuse in Cleveland (Parton and Reid, 2017). The 'Cleveland Inquiry' highlighted a number of concerns, in particular that professionals, through their work in supporting families and providing strategies for intervention, had been overzealous and acted in a potentially inappropriate way. Working Together in 1988, therefore, aimed to guide professionals in their work but also afford families an element of privacy.

The Children Act 1989 necessitated further revisions of the Working Together guidance and the 1999 revision clarified the differentiation between safeguarding and child protection, focusing on arrangements for interagency working. The document emphasised a subtle change in practice for children's services; not only did it highlight the need for agencies to work in partnership but also for practitioners who were directed to assess children's needs and consider any impairment that might affect their development. A further modification in 2006 followed the publication of the Every Child Matters Green Paper in 2003 and the subsequent 2004 Children Act, and was introduced to take account of the Laming report into the death of Victoria Climbie (Parton and Reid, 2017).

An inquiry and serious case review following the death of Peter Connelly aged 17 months in Haringey further strengthened the guidance in 2010. Parton and Reid (2017) note the increased complexity of this version, as it attempted to reflect concerns about the management of serious case reviews and clarify practitioner responsibilities. The document included a new chapter that aimed to inform practitioners on a number of issues relating to safeguarding and promoting the welfare of children in the following specialist areas.

- sexually exploited children
- gang activity
- fabricated illness
- complex organised or multiple abuse

- female genital mutilation
- forced marriage or honour based violence
- allegations of abuse made against a person who works with children
- abuse of disabled children
- child abuse linked to 'spirit possession'
- child victims of trafficking.

(HM Government, 2010, chapter 6 pp. 191–204)

In 2013, the revised version, published under the Coalition Government, highlighted the importance of keeping the child at the centre of practice. Informed by Professor Eileen Munro's report, recommendations were made to revise child protection systems, reduce bureaucracy and focus on the needs of children (DfE, 2013). The current 2015 version of Working Together to Safeguard Children was updated in 2017 to take account of new guidance on the definition of child sexual exploitation. A further review is forthcoming; this follows legislative changes in the Children and Social Work Act 2017. What appears to be important is that revisions are made to statutory guidance following significant events that impact on practice with children, further confirming the need for practitioners to be vigilant and mindful.

ACTIVITY

There have been many revisions to the Working Together to Safeguard Children (WTSC) guidance, each one highlighted the importance of being vigilant.

1   List each one and write a sentence to describe how this knowledge will impact on your practice.
2   Make a note in your diary to keep up to date with the Department for Education website so that you are aware when the new version of WTSC is published; what key messages can you identify in the new guidance?
3   How will this new guidance inform your studies and practice?

The Children and Social Work Act 2017 has already started to have a significant impact on the way local authorities carry out their work. The Act details amendments to the 2004 Children Act including a change to the arrangements for partnership working between agencies. The new legislation will see Local Safeguarding Children Boards replaced with Child Safeguarding Review Panels and Serious Case Reviews renamed Child Death Reviews. A number of other reforms relate to the provision for children who are looked after by the local authority, care leavers, sex education through Personal Social Health Education (PSHE) and the way the social work profession operates.

Despite these changes there are a number of significant documents that contain key pieces of legislation and essential aspects that you need to be familiar with. Early years providers must comply, under section 40 of the Childcare Act 2006; these requirements are clearly set out in the Early Years Foundation Stage document (HM Government, 2015a; DfE, 2017).

Key documents

The following list of documents whilst not exhaustive contains advice and guidance for practitioners working in ECEC:

- The Early Years Foundation Stage (EYFS) (DfE, 2017)
- Working Together to Safeguard Children. A guide to interagency working to safeguard and promote the welfare of children (HM Government, 2015a)
- What to do if you are worried a child is being abused. Advice for practitioners (HM Government, 2015b)
- Protecting children from radicalisation: the prevent duty (DfE, 2015)
- Keeping children safe in education: for schools and colleges (DfE, 2016).

You have a duty of care to the children you work with, which means that you have a responsibility to promote good health and protect children from harm (DfE, 2017, p. 16). The Children Act 1989 together with the United Nations Convention on the Rights of the Child (UNCRC; UNICEF, 1989) underpin the need to respect the rights of children in relation to the provision of services for children. Together with partners in other children's services you have a responsibility to ensure children are at the centre of practice, and this includes making sure their individual needs are met and taking time to consider their wishes and feelings (HM Government, 2015a).

THINKING ACTIVITY

- Spend some time researching current safeguarding documents. The National Society for the Prevention of Cruelty to Children, NSPCC and Department for Education will be good places to start.
- Why is it important that you keep yourself up to date with changes in legislation?
- Consider and make a list of your training to date. Is there anything further you can access?

What to do if you are worried – your role

The safeguarding and welfare requirements in the EYFS directs practitioners to 'take all necessary steps'; this means practitioners must ensure children are kept safe inside and outside the setting and that consideration is given to make sure their health needs are met (DfE, 2017, p. 16). As a student you will become aware of the various responsibilities your colleagues undertake in their daily duties. Although it is unlikely that you will assume full responsibility, it is expected that you will gain, during your training, experience at a more senior level. Understanding the role of the senior or lead practitioner will prepare you for future roles and you may well find that you are expected to be responsible for a particular age group or room of children who attend the provision. This may also include working more formally alongside the designated safeguarding lead. All settings must have a named and deputy designated lead person on the premises at all times.

The EYFS 3.5 states:

> A practitioner must be designated to take the lead responsibility for safeguarding children in every setting. The lead practitioner is responsible for liaison with local statutory children's services agencies, and with the Local Safeguarding Children Board (LSCB). They must provide support and guidance to other staff on an ongoing basis.
>
> (DfE, 2017 p. 16)

The safeguarding lead is therefore a significant role in the setting and one that offers support, advice and guidance to other staff members. The role also requires the practitioner to attend an appropriate level of training that is updated on a regular basis (DfE, 2017; HM Government, 2015a).

There are four key steps (Figure 6.1) to help you identify and respond appropriately when you are concerned about a child, and while it is not essential to follow the steps chronologically you must act if you believe a child is at risk of harm or in danger (HM Government, 2015b). What is of paramount importance is the need to keep comprehensive records, documenting all concerns, discussions and decisions.

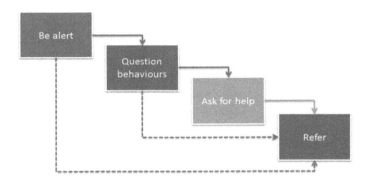

Figure 6.1 Steps to identify abuse and/or neglect.
Adapted from HM Government (2015b).

ACTIVITY

You are working alongside your mentor, who is also the designated safeguarding lead. A member of the baby room staff team comes to see your mentor to explain that she is worried about one of her key children who is 18 months. The practitioner has spoken to the child's mother about repeated nappy rash and lack of adequate clothing but today has concerns that the child is also very hungry.

- Following the four steps in Figure 6.1, what would your course of action be?
- When would you talk to the child's parent?
- What support could you offer the family?

Challenges facing children and families

There has been a myriad of policies and initiatives aimed at improving services for children over the last 50 years, however, the National Children's Bureau (NCB) suggests children, especially those with multiple disadvantages, continue to miss out on the support they need (NCB, 2017). Children's life chances are affected by social, political and economic experiences and although past governments have focused heavily on improving social mobility, for some children and families many challenges remain. The current government in 2015 redefined their commitment to improving social mobility and raised the issue of parenting as a key factor in improving opportunities and reducing inequalities (Family and Childcare Trust, 2015).

Parenting and the role parents and carers play in children's lives continues to be a contentious topic, and whether parenting is a matter for political debate or personal to families has long been disputed. The early years matter and according to the Social Mobility Commission (SMC), less than half of disadvantaged children are school ready by the age of five (SMC, 2017). The quality of parenting can have an impact on early child development as it is through their early interactions that children gain the foundations for future learning (Family and Childcare Trust, 2015; NCB, 2017). The importance of good quality services for children and families can make a difference, nonetheless, government spending has been squeezed in recent years and children's services have felt the impact of this (Family and Childcare Trust, 2015).

In the current financial climate, doing more with less has become a mantra, and practitioners in health, education and wider family services will be familiar with the expectation placed upon them to improve outcomes for children through integrated working. Practitioners in the early years are well placed to work in an integrated way, focusing on working in partnership with parents, liaising with health and family support agencies and supporting the home learning environment.

Intervening early

Settings that provide early education and child care have the potential to support families through early intervention. They play a fundamental role in the provision of universal children's services and together with health services they are often at the forefront of practice, caring for society's youngest children and their families. All children have an entitlement to access universal children's services during their early years, and services must, according to Tickell (2011), have a clear strategy to support child development. As early years services in England are offered by a diverse number of childcare/early years settings (Dyer and McMahon, 2018), practitioners need to find ways to develop and commit to universal practice by working together and taking every opportunity to put children at the centre of their practice.

Universal early years services became a statutory duty in the Childcare Act 2006; sections 20 and 96 (6) placed a responsibility on all local authorities in England to provide early years provision for children from birth to 5 years (DCSF, 2010). The Act also introduced the sufficiency duty, which directed every local authority to provide high quality, flexible and affordable childcare (DSCF, 2010). This duty was further extended in the Education Act 2011 to ensure local authorities provide up to 15 hours of funding for 3- and 4-year-olds. In 2013 this was extended to include 20%

of the most disadvantaged 2-year-olds in England identified through an assessment of household income. This targeted intervention is seen an opportunity to provide young children with quality childcare and also to enable the early identification of special educational needs (DfE and DH, 2011).

The focus on disadvantage coincided with the launch of the Equality Act 2010 and intensified with the publication of a number of influential reports commissioned and presented to the Coalition Government. Reports by Sir Michael Marmot (2010), Frank Field MP (2010), Graham Allen MP (2011), Dame Claire Tickell (2011) and Professor Eileen Munro (2011) highlighted the importance of addressing inequalities in society. Early years practice was particularly influenced through a focus on inequalities in health and education by providing help for families through early intervention as this was perceived to benefit children cognitively and emotionally (DfE and DH, 2011). In September 2014 under the remit of the Coalition Government, the 2-year-old offer was extended further to provide nursery education for the 40% most disadvantaged 2-year-olds. The promotion of the offer was further supported by the Effective Provision of Pre-School Education (EPPE) research that suggested early education before children are three has the potential to impact on children's future cognitive outcomes (Siraj-Blatchford et al., 2008).

Georgeson et al. (2014) describe the potential impact of this policy on early intervention, particularly as in the following September, 2014, this policy extended further to enable 40% of the most disadvantaged 2-year-olds to access funding. Funding has continued and is now legislated in the 2016 Childcare Act. With the current pre-school offer for all 3- and 4-year-olds and some 2-year-olds to have an entitlement of 15 hours of funded early education (DfE, 2014), settings are well placed to impact on the welfare of all children who attend and are key players in ensuring children are safeguarded and protected from harm.

ACTIVITY

Consider how the presence of 2-year-olds in early years settings have impacted on provision. Do you have targeted interventions at your disposal to offer support for families, perhaps working with colleagues in health services?

With many settings providing services for 2-year-olds there is a need to ensure the environment is able to meet the unique needs of such young children.

How might you create an enabling environment for 2-year-olds?
What might you need to include in your provision?
How will you work with parents and carers to develop a suitable accessible environment?

Child centred practice

It is important to make sure adults do not become a barrier to protecting children and whilst it acknowledged that strong working partnerships are important, practitioners must be aware of the necessity to keep the child's needs at the forefront of their practice. This is illustrated by the work of Munro, commissioned in 2010 to undertake an independent review of child protection, by the Secretary of State for Education. Munro focused her work on protecting vulnerable children and investigating practice; her final report, in 2011, announced a number of recommendations aimed at clarifying professional accountability and encouraging shared responsibility (Munro, 2011). Of particular interest and of concern to early years practitioners is the emphasis on child-centred practice.

Child centred practice is reinforced in the EYFS and practitioners are expected to support the development of each child as an individual (DfE, 2017). Understanding the concept of the unique child being supported and nurtured, is a fundamental characteristic in practice with the role of the practitioner as key person essential in creating an ethos where children are respected and their rights supported.

The EYFS 3.27 states that:

> Each child must be assigned a key person. Their role is to help ensure that every child's care is tailored to meet their individual needs, to help the child become familiar with the setting, offer a settled relationship for the child and build a relationship with the parents.

> (DfE, 2017, p. 22)

The EYFS also requires practitioners, parents and carers to work in partnership (DfE, 2017). The key person is, therefore, the one person who is able to identify and attend to the needs of both the child and the parent. The best interests of children must be regarded by all adults who care for them (UNCRC, 1989). This can be challenging for practitioners, as behaviours and requests from parents and carers may seem to contradict what the practitioner believes is in the child's best interests. It is important that there are support mechanisms in place to enable communication with managers and senior practitioners.

THINKING ACTIVITY

You are asked by a parent of one of your key children to make sure they do not sleep during the afternoon. The parent works full time and has explained that they are very busy and that they need to make sure their child is able to go to bed when they get home. In recent days the child has been tired, they are only 18 months and you feel that having a sleep is necessary. They have a long day in nursery and developmentally you feel an afternoon is not unreasonable. However, as key person you have a responsibility to work in partnership with the parents and also make sure the child's needs are being met.

How does this situation make you feel?
What can you offer the parents?
What can you do to ensure you meet the child's needs?

Disguised compliance

In some cases, working with parents and carers can become even more complicated; balancing the needs of the child and adults can cause conflict to the detriment of both parties, but particularly the child. Disguised compliance is a term used to define behaviour where adults caring for children appear to cooperate and have regard for the child's welfare but their behaviour or actions suggest otherwise. Disguised compliance can be summed up as behaviour which is adopted by adults to avoid suspicion of harming a child and which is intended to deflect professional concerns (Reder, Duncan and Gray, 1993). Simply put, parents and carers could appear to be concerned and working in partnership with practitioners in order to prevent further investigation of a safeguarding concern or hide any actual significant harm to a child.

A number of serious case reviews have highlighted the need for practitioners to be aware of the concept of disguised compliance as opportunities to eliminate risk can be missed when attention is deflected from the original source of concern. Practitioners have a duty to keep children at the centre of their concern and minimise the risk of harm (HM Government, 2015a); disguised compliance can result when practitioners are overly optimistic about progress or lose sight of the child's needs. Missing opportunities to make timely interventions has resulted in disguised compliance being cited as a factor in many cases where children have been subjected to significant harm or have died (NSPCC, 2014).

As early years practitioners, it is your responsibility to work alongside agencies and lead professionals and sharing information will be essential practice, therefore, being aware of your own responsibilities and those of others, especially parents and carers is essential. The following case study will help you to understand disguised compliance. The case study concludes with a number of questions that are intended to challenge your thinking.

Case study

Emily is 2 years old, she lives with her mother, Gemma, and two brothers Danny aged 4 years and Drew aged 6 years in a privately rented flat. Danny and Drew do not see their father but Emily's father occasionally stays in the family home. The family have been on the radar of services for a number of years as there have been previous concerns about neglect and all three children living in the family home have recently been put on a child protection plan. A number of issues have been highlighted including the poor conditions of the home, continued untidiness including dirty nappies left strewn in the garden, food on the floor and unclean bedding. Danny, Drew and Emily have continual head lice. The family have had sporadic engagement with services, and visits by professionals have often been unsuccessful due to the family being out. The boys' attendance at school is hit and miss. Gemma does however attend all the intervention meetings she is invited to, she attended initial early intervention meetings and the subsequent Initial Child Protection Conference. She has also attended follow up meetings, where she agreed to actions concerning improving living conditions and engagement with professionals.

Emily has started to attend your setting, funded by the '2-year-old' offer; you are assigned as her key person and have had regular updates from Gemma's social worker and health visitor. Gemma does engage with you and often spends time talking to you about the improvements she is making in the family home. However, you are aware that the health visitor has tried to make a number of home visits and the social worker has shared with you that there are still major concerns. You are also aware that there will be a Case Conference review within the month.

1   What are the dilemmas and challenges for you when working with Gemma?
2   How do you ensure that you follow child centred practice at all times?
3   What is your responsibility to other agencies?
4   What might you need to consider when preparing for the forthcoming conference meeting?

Contemporary challenges

Safeguarding is everyone's responsibility (HM Government, 2015a) and familiarity with contemporary challenges and the need to safeguard children in early years are well documented. All staff working in children's services should have an awareness of safeguarding issues; however, there are some specific duties that practitioners working in education and early years settings must be aware of (DfE, 2016; DfE 2017). Alongside providing a safe environment and offering help early when needed, practitioners need to be aware of policies that cover the use of mobile phones and cameras, including sharing inappropriate images. All early education providers must consider the increasing element of digital technologies and the impact of this on the role of the early years practitioner, and the children they work with.

Digital safeguarding responsibilities

As an early years practitioner, you have a number of safeguarding responsibilities, including collecting, storing and sharing information about children and their families. Within settings, this information is required to be safely and efficiently managed and is often digitalised within administrative or working documents, such as observations and photos, as part of online learning journeys, used to assess children's needs holistically (DfE, 2017, p 31). Practitioners must be aware of the legal framework for confidentiality, which can be found in the Data Protection Act 1998 and the Freedom of Information Act 2000, which all staff are required to accept responsibility for to provide safe and effective data management (DfE, 2017, p 32; Savage and Barnett, 2017).

THINKING ACTIVITY

- How would you rate your own digital literacy and how does this influence your practice?
- Reflect on your recent digital practices ... how do you think this impacts on the children you work with?

Ethical considerations

As an early years practitioner, you need to be aware of the risks and benefits of engaging with digital technology, helping to provide a constructive environment where staff, children and families keep themselves and others safe (Ofsted, 2016). Ofsted (2016) provide clear guidance for early years settings, suggesting, 'leaders oversee the safe use of technology when children and learners are in their care and take action immediately if they are concerned about bullying or children's well-being' (p. 8), whilst also implementing the 'required policies with regard to the safe use of mobile phones and cameras in settings' (p. 8). As an early years student, you may also need to consider ethics within a digitally submitted assignment, where you are often asked to reflect on your practice, or perhaps you have gathered data for a research project; here privacy, confidentiality and anonymity are crucial.

Digital footprints

With the growth of online communication and social media, you must consider your own digital footprint and those of the children you work with. Thatcher (2014) defines a digital footprint as the information and data that people generate, through purposive action or passive recording, when they go online. As an early years practitioner, you need to consider what you share professionally online, in keeping with the setting's policies and what happens to this information once shared. As discussed, there are laws to protect children's rights and privacy within professional settings; however, with the availability of screenshot technology, any information viewed is easily copied, raising ethical questions around confidentiality and privacy. Information is often shared with parents, who are presumed to be the most effective guardians to safeguard their children's private information, yet the increase of 'sharenting', a term used to describe the ways many parents share details about their children's lives online, potentially suggests conflict between children's privacy rights and their opportunity to impact on their own digital footprints (Stienberg, 2017). As a practitioner, you may need to consider the digital literacy of parents, as research shows this is linked to how they manage their own and their child's digital engagement, involving parents in discussions about online safety to potentially safeguard children's digital footprint and providing guidance on how to share safely (Lou et al., 2010).

ACTIVITY

Thinking about your digital footprint, search for yourself online, what information is publicly available?

- Consider the information publicly available about you, how does this reflect on your professionalism?
- Remember, you may get potential employers or parents searching for information about you online; you need to continuously monitor your online presence.

Younger children and the digital technology debate

Digital technologies increasingly affect the lives of younger children, who are accessing digital technologies at an increasingly early age and for longer periods of time (Mekinc, Smailbegovic and Kokic, 2013). However, research identifies that some parents and practitioners are anxious about how younger children engage with digital technologies, suggesting that this is an area of contemporary consideration within early childhood education (Chaudron, 2015; Savage and Barnett, 2017). Younger children within early years settings are often at the forefront of technologies, raising questions over how they are viewed, either as passive participants requiring safeguarding and protection, or active participants requiring guidance. What is clear is that these early experiences with technology have been identified as a crucial period in younger children gaining an understanding of the safe use of technology and its associated risks as they move through the education system further beyond the influence of adults (Ito, Davidson and Jenkins, 2008; Livingstone and Third, 2017). The increased digitalisation of society potentially requires us to re-examine past notions of childhood and consider how technology has, does and will impact on children's lives, possibly calling for a continuous shift in cultural attitudes around early years practice and safeguarding in a digital world.

The role of supervision in supporting practice

Working with children can be a rewarding but challenging profession; the EYFS acknowledges that practitioners have appropriate qualifications, knowledge, skills and experience. Furthermore, it also offers additional guidance on the support staff should receive in order to manage complex family situations, ensuring staff receive regular training to help them understand their roles and responsibilities (DfE, 2017). Additionally, the EYFS asks that staff receive regular supervision in order to evaluate and analyse their practice with children and families.

The EYFS states 3.21:

> Effective supervision provides, support, coaching and training for the practitioner and promotes the interests of children. Supervision should foster a culture of mutual support, teamwork and continuous improvement, which encourages the confidential discussion of sensitive issues.
>
> (DfE, 2017 p. 21)

The initial Statutory Framework for the EYFS in 2008 discussed the need for staff appraisal and continual professional development, however, supervision as a practice recommendation was introduced in the 2012 revision of the EYFS, following recommendations in the 2011 Tickell review. Supervision, although relatively new in the early years profession, is long embedded in the health and social care professions. Professional supervision as the name suggests involves the management and regulation of professional activity, in health care, often called clinical supervision, it is described as 'protection for the client and education for the professional' (Royal College of Nursing, 2018).

Supervision in social care, suggests Morrison (2005), is the process of enhancing the skills of the professional in order to achieve competency in practice; good practice should ensure positive outcomes for both the worker and users of services. Both professions discuss the practice as providing opportunities to develop an organisational culture that values both the people it serves and its employees. It should be reflective and reflexive and an emotionally safe environment for staff to have discussions and make decisions (SCIE, 2017). Effective supervision for early years practitioners, it could be argued, is a combination of both the above; practitioners are encouraged to reflect on their practice as this process offers practitioners the opportunity to evaluate their actions (Johns, 2009).

THINKING ACTIVITY

Consider the possibility of co-working a key group of children with your mentor and discussing each child, their family circumstances and identifying needs. The meeting offers the opportunity for your to discuss practice and think of ways to support each child, liaise with their parent/carers and any other appropriate agencies.

Drawing on John's structured reflective model can you imagine how you would think about each child's specific circumstances?

Johns Model of Reflection

Describe the experience – what were the significant factors?
Reflect – what were you trying to achieve and what were the consequences?
What were the influencing factors – internal/external/knowledge that affected decisions?
What could have been done differently, what other choices did I have?
What have I learned, what will change because of this experience?

(Adapted from Johns, 2009)

Conclusion

This chapter encouraged you to consider safeguarding and the welfare of children as you become more proficient in both your knowledge and skills. Legislation explored alongside your developing role challenged you to consider early years practice as an integral aspect of early intervention. Contemporary issues were offered as examples to encourage you to reflect on practice. This chapter cannot replace official documents, merely highlight the need to be vigilant and proactive and act at all times in the best interest of the child.

Additional reading

Burton, S. and Reid, J. (Eds) (2017) *Safeguarding and protecting children in the early years.* Available at: https://ebookcentral.proquest.com (accessed 26 March 2018).
National Children's Bureau (2017) Off the radar: shining the light on children whose rights and welfare are at risk. London: National Children's Bureau.

Bibliography

Allen, G. (2011) *Early intervention: the next steps*. London: H M Government. Available at: www.gov.uk/government/uploads/system/uploads/attachment_data/file/284086/early-intervention-next-steps2.pdf (accessed 26 March 2018).

Burton, S. and Reid, J. (Eds) (2017) *Safeguarding and protecting children in the early years*. Available at: https://ebookcentral.proquest.com (accessed 26 March 2018).

Chaudron, S. (2015) Young children (0–8) and digital technology: a qualitative exploratory study across seven countries. Ispra: Joint Research centre – European commission.

Department for Children Schools and Families (DCSF) (2010).Securing sufficient childcare: statutory guidance for local authorities in carrying out their childcare sufficiency duties. Crown Copyright: DSCF-00274–2010.

Department for Education and Department of Health (DfE and DH) (2011) *Supporting families in the foundation years*. Crown copyright. Available at: www.gov.uk/government/uploads/system/uploads/attachment_data/file/184868/DFE-01001-2011_supporting_families_in_the_foundation_years.pdf (accessed 26 March 2018).

Department for Education (DfE) (2013) *Statement from Edward Timpson about the publication of the revised statutory guidance 'Working together to safeguard children'*. Available at: www.gov.uk/government/speeches/working-together-to-safeguard-children (accessed 26 March 2018).

Department for Education (DfE) (2014). Early education and childcare: statutory guidance for local authorities. London: DfE.

Department for *Education* (DfE) (2015) *The Prevent duty departmental advice for schools and childcare providers*. Crown Copyright. Available at: www.gov.uk/government/uploads/system/uploads/attachment_data/file/439598/prevent-duty-departmental-advice-v6.pdf (accessed 26 March 2018).

Department for Education (DfE) (2016) *Keeping children safe in education: for schools and colleges*. London: DfE. Available at: www.gov.uk/government/uploads/system/uploads/attachment_data/file/550511/Keeping_children_safe_in_education.pdf (accessed 26 March 2018).

Department for Education (DfE) (2017) Statutory framework for the early years foundation stage. Setting the standards for learning, development and care for children from birth to five, Manchester: Department for Education.

Dyer, M. and McMahon, S. (2017) Work-based practice in the early years: a guide for students. Oxon: Routledge.

Dyer, M. and McMahon, S. (2018) Development of the early years sector. In McMahon, S. and Dyer, M. (2018) Work-based practice in the early years: a guide for students. Oxon: Routledge

Family and Childcare Trust (2015) *The Parliamentary Inquiry into Parenting and social mobility: enhancing parenting across the UK*. Available at: www.familyandchildcaretrust.org/parliamentary-inquiry-parenting-and-social-mobility (accessed 27 March 2018).

Field, F. (2010) *The foundation years: preventing poor children becoming poor adults*. London: HM Government. Available at: http://webarchive.nationalarchives.gov.uk/20110120090141/http://povertyreview.independent.gov.uk/media/20254/poverty-report.pdf (accessed 27 March 2018).

Georgeson, J., Campbell-Barr, V., Mathers, S., Boag-Munroe, G., Parker-Rees, R. and Caruso, F. (2014) *Two-year-olds in England: an exploratory study*. Plymouth University and Oxford University. Available at: http://tactyc.org.uk/wp-content/uploads/2014/11/TACTYC_2_year_olds_Report_2014.pdf (accessed 26 March 2018).

HM Government (2010) *Working together to safeguard children. A guide to inter-agency working to safeguard and promote the welfare of children*. Available at: www.safeguardinginschools.co.uk/wp-content/uploads/2015/04/Working-Together-2010-Training-Groups.pdf (accessed 26 March 2018).

HM Government (2015a) *Working together to safeguard children. A guide to inter-agency working to safeguard and promote the welfare of children.* London: Crown Copyright. Available at: www.gov.uk/government/uploads/system/uploads/attachment_data/file/592101/Working_Together_to_Safeguard_Children_20170213.pdf (accessed 26 March 2018).

HM Government (2015b) What to do if you are worried a child is being abused. Advice for practitioners. London: Crown Copyright

Ito, M., Davidson C. and Jenkins, H. (2008) Foreword. In Buckingham D (ed.) *Youth, identity, digital media* (pp. vii–ix). Cambridge, MA; London: The MIT Press.

Johns, C. (2009) *Becoming a reflective practitioner.* 3rd edn. Oxford: Blackwell Publishing.

Livingstone, S. and Third, A. (2017) Children and young people's rights in the digital age: an emerging agenda. *New Media and Society,* 19 (5), 657–670. doi:10.1177/1461444816686318

Lou, S., Shih, R., Liu, H., Guo, Y. and Tseng, K. (2010) The influences of the sixth graders' parents' internet literacy and parenting style on internet parenting. *The Turkish Online Journal of Educational Technology,* 9 (4), 173–184.

Marmot, M. (2010) *Fair society, healthy lives: the Marmot Review: strategic review of health inequalities in England post-2010.* ISBN 9780956487001. Available at: www.gov.uk/dfid-research-outputs/fair-society-healthy-lives-the-marmot-review-strategic-review-of-health-inequalities-in-england-post-2010 (accessed 26 March 2018).

Mekinc, J., Smailbegovic, T. and Kokic, A. (2013) Should we be concerned about Children using the internet? – Pilot study. *Innovative Issues and Approaches in Social Sciences,* 6 (2), 6–20.

Morrison, T. (2005). *Staff supervision in social care.* Brighton: Pavilion.

Munro, E. (2011) The Munro review of child protection: final report. A child-centred system. London. The Stationery Office.

National Children's Bureau (NCB) (2017) Off the radar: shining the light on children whose rights and welfare are at risk. London: National Children's Bureau.

National Society for the Prevention of Cruelty to Children (NSPCC) (2014) Disguised compliance: learning from case reviews. Summary of risk factors and learning for improved practice around families and disguised compliance. Available at: www.nspcc.org.uk/preventing-abuse/child-protection-system/case-reviews/learning/disguised-compliance/ (accessed 26 March 2018).

Ofsted (2016) Inspecting safeguarding in early years, education and skills settings. Guidance for inspectors undertaking inspection under the common inspection framework. Manchester: Ofsted.

Parton, N. and Reid, J. (2017) The recent history of central government and guidance about child protection. In Burton, S. and Reid, J. (Eds), *Safeguarding and protecting children in the early years.* Available at: https://ebookcentral.proquest.com (accessed 27 March 2018).

Reder, P., Duncan, S. and Gray, M. (1993) *Beyond blame: child abuse tragedies revisited.* London: Routledge.

Royal College of Nursing (RCN) (2018) *Clinical supervision.* Available at: www.rcn.org.uk/get-help/rcn-advice/clinical-supervision (accessed 27 March 2018).

Savage, M. and Barnett, A. (2017) *Technology-enhanced learning in the early years foundation stage.* St Albans: Critical Publishing.

Siraj-Blatchford, I., Taggart, B., Sylva, K., Sammons, P. and Melhuish, E. (2008) Towards the transformation of practice in early childhood education: the effective provision of pre-school education (EPPE) project. *Cambridge Journal of Education,* 38 (1), 23–36. 10.1080/03057640801889956.

Social Care Institute for Excellence (SCIE) (2017). *Effective supervision in a variety of settings, SCIE Guide 50.* Available at: www.scie.org.uk/publications/guide50/index.asp (accessed 27 March 2018).

Social Mobility Commission (SMC) (2017) *State of the nation 2017: social mobility in Great Britain*. Crown Copyright. Available at: www.gov.uk/government/publications (accessed 27 March 2018).

Steinberg, S.B. (2017) Sharenting: children's privacy in the age of social media. *Emory Law Journal*, 66 (4), 839.

Thatcher, J. (2014) Living on fumes: digital footprints, data fumes, and the limitations of spatial big data. *International Journal of Communication*, 8, 1765–1783.

Tickell, C. (2011) A review into the impact of the early years foundation stage (EYFS) on children's learning and development, and early years practitioners. London: Department for Education.

UNICEF (1989) *The United Nations Convention on the Rights of the Child*. London: UNICEF. Available at: www.unicef.org.uk/Documents/Publication-pdfs/UNCRC_PRESS200910web.pdf (accessed 27 March 2018).

Chapter 7

A creative curriculum

Alison Ryan

> **CHAPTER AIMS**
>
> By the end of this chapter you will:
>
> - have an understanding of the creative curriculum
> - have developed an understanding of the wider early years curriculum
> - know how you can support children's development through cross curricular and thematic learning
> - be aware of how observation and assessment can be used to support your practice
> - be able to start to evaluate your own planning.

What is a creative curriculum?

A creative curriculum is focused on the child and the whole of the child's development, not just in core subjects such as literacy and maths but in arts, humanities and sciences as well. There are many different views on what these curricula will look like in practice but all contain key themes:

- Child centred and inclusive practice
- An emphasis on skills above knowledge
- Time is given to consolidate learning
- Creativity is a central feature.

(Burgess, 2007)

Early education should focus on children being able to explore their ideas through play which enables them to develop their creativity as well as thinking and problem solving skills. The EYFS framework (DfE, 2017) is based around the idea of play being essential in this development and that should be the way children learn before moving on to some formal aspects of learning in the Key Stage 1 curriculum, at the age of 5. It has been argued that children should still have access to a wider play based and more creative curriculum until the age of 6 (Rose, 2009); however the recent reforms of Key Stage 1 assessment in 2016 have led to an increasing focus in some schools on literacy and maths in preparation for SATs tests at the age of 7. Schools based on Montessori and Steiner principles have different approaches to the curriculum with more emphasis on a holistic, artistic and cultural curriculum (Kirkham and Kidd, 2017).

What do we mean by creativity within the curriculum?

Bruce (2011, p. 5) says that 'The imagination makes images in the mind. Creativity is the process by which children turn these images into creations'. Often practitioners may think they are not creative themselves, thinking about their own experiences of formal learning in art and related subjects at school. However, creativity is more than just the technical skills of being good at things like drawing and the ability to play instruments. It is about thinking in an imaginative way and it is about seeing imaginative play in the most ordinary of objects. Children are naturally imaginative as they have not yet learnt the rules for what things are, they are not constrained by knowing the labels, uses and purposes of things. To a 3-year-old a box has endless possibilities, it is not just a container, it can be a multitude of things and the fact that it may be undecorated and uninspiring for an adult to look at does not prevent them from turning it into a home for a dinosaur, a ship to sail around the world or a cave for the Gruffalo. Their imagination gives them to ability to transform the everyday into the amazing. The key focus for children is the freedom to play and develop their own creativity.

Play

Play has many benefits for children, it helps them develop their thinking and explore new ideas and situations. It can help to develop their use of symbols to make sense of the world and to understand how other people think and behave (Bruce, 2011). A key component of a creative curriculum is giving children the opportunity to explore different aspects of their world through play.

THINKING ACTIVITY

Think about what toys you played with when you were younger, if you cannot remember you may have pictures of you with favourite toys or can ask a relative.

What is the difference between the toys available then and now?

What were your experiences of creative play i.e. building dens, creating your own spaces to play rather than being given things to use?

Outdoor learning

For many settings a creative curriculum is one that makes full use of outdoor learning opportunities. This will vary depending on the location of the setting and for some settings it will mean access to areas that are already suitable for a Forest Schools approach; for others it will be the use of existing play areas that can be developed to enable creative play and for the environment to be used to its full potential. This does not mean having lots of fixed equipment such as climbing frames and play areas and 'playtime' scheduled for certain times of the day but to use the outdoor environment for learning for as much time as the indoor.

Forest Schools

The links between the Forest School ethos and the creative curriculum can be clearly seen in two of the principles from the Forest School Association.

> Forest School uses a range of learner-centred processes to create a community for being, development and learning.
> Forest School aims to promote the holistic development of all those involved, fostering resilient, confident, independent and creative learners.
> (Forest School Association, 2017)

Forest Schools originated from early work by practitioners to develop alternative approaches to education and are based on longstanding principles of outdoor education but have been very much inspired by the approach to early years education in Scandinavian countries. The Forest School ethos is one that is outlined by this statement from Knight (2011, p. 4), 'learning is as far as possible initiated by the participants, centred on their needs and playful', linking very clearly with the role of play. Forest School experiences are designed to be repeated over a longer period of time than just the occasional walk in the woods to enable children to really get to know the environment by exploring, again linking to the idea of time being needed to consolidate learning.

Loose parts play

Loose parts play is play with objects that can be combined in any number of different ways and offer children the chance to really use their imagination. Unlike commercially available toys for children, including those that do have creative elements such as Duplo, Lego and blockplay, the material used in loose parts play offers endless possibilities. Loose parts are things such as sticks, stones, pine cones, buildings materials such as planks and tubes and scrapyard/found material such as tyres. These are the sorts of things that children have been playing with for generations, often as there were few other resources for them to play with. Since many children now have a wealth of other play options to choose from these may have been forgotten about and their potential missed. Loose parts play is normally outdoor play but can be used indoors as well, particularly with the smaller resources.

The benefits of loose parts play are varied but can be explained by this quote.

> When children interact with loose parts, they enter a world of 'what if' that promotes the type of thinking that leads to problem solving and theoretical reasoning. Loose parts enhance children's ability to think imaginatively and see solutions, and they bring a sense of adventure and excitement to children's play.
> (Daly and Beloglovsky, 2015, cited in Casey and Robertson, 2016, p. 11)

There are many toys that have been developed that offer creative opportunities but the real value of the resources for loose parts play is in their variety. There may be no uniform size or shape to them so unlike a Duplo or Lego set where everything will fit together because it has been designed to do so children will have to be more creative if they want to build something with their loose parts. Loose parts play involves experimenting, thinking about the properties of materials and asking questions such as 'is that strong enough?', 'how can we make that taller?'. In this way it links back to both the skill development and the creativity themes of a creative curriculum. As loose parts play often takes place outdoors and involves the construction of dens, walkways and other structures it helps with the development of physical aspects such as co-ordination, balance and all important communication and co-operative play.

ACTIVITY

Look for examples of children being creative within their play in your setting. They may be taking an object and using it in a different way or talking about imaginary situations.

Try and determine what has inspired them to do this; it may have been a story they have heard or something they have observed in their own lives.

Planning creatively and planning for creativity

When thinking about how to plan for a creative curriculum it is useful to start by thinking about the different aspects of the curriculum for children 0–5 years old and for 5–7 years of age when they move into Key Stage 1.

The EYFS framework (DfE, 2017) covers seven areas of learning and development, the first three areas being referred to as the prime areas due to their importance underpinning all other learning:

- personal, social, emotional development
- communication and language
- physical development
- literacy
- mathematics
- understanding the world
- expressive arts and design.

The National Curriculum (DfE, 2016) also consists of 'core subjects' of English, mathematics and science, and the, 'foundation subjects', which are:

- art and design
- computing (ICT)
- design and technology
- geography
- history

- music
- physical education.

In addition to this schools also need to teach religious education, Personal, Social and Health Education,(PSHE) and citizenship. There are Key Skills which are not assessed, which include:

- communication
- application of number
- information technology
- working with others
- improving own learning and performance
- problem solving and thinking skills, covering information-processing, reasoning, enquiry, creative thinking and evaluation skills.

There are also five cross-curricular elements in Key Stage 1, which means that these should be considered in all taught subjects; these are:

- creativity
- ICT
- education for sustainable development
- literacy across the curriculum
- numeracy across the curriculum.

If we were to think about trying to teach all of these things separately we would have to spend only a small amount of time on each session and not only would that lead to very fragmented learning for the children but also would not reflect the real life skills that people use. Young children need time to absorb what they are doing and to not only develop specific skills such as communication but also learn how and when to apply those skills. This links back to the key themes from a creative curriculum of developing skills rather than knowledge and giving children time to consolidate their learning.

Therefore, it makes sense not only for the practitioners but also for the child that learning is planned in a way that links together all of the important aspects of learning at whatever stage they are at. It is important to remember that as a practitioner you are aware of all the different sections of the EYFS or Key Stage 1 curriculum but young children do not see learning as something that needs to be split into separate sections. Having gone through secondary and further education with its division of learning into separate subjects taught by different teachers it is often challenging to think about planning in a cross curricular way rather than planning for a particular area of the EYFS or the Key Stage 1 curriculum. As creative practitioners we need to look for ways to draw all of these aspects together and to not only plan creatively to meet outcomes but allow our planning to be focused on starting where the child is, rather than looking at the outcomes that they have to meet. This is central to meeting the key theme of child centred and inclusive practice in a creative curriculum.

We also need to give children lots of opportunity to develop their own creativity through everything that we plan. This may mean that the end result of an activity is not we what thought it would be as the child's imagination may take them in a different direction. As adults we are sometimes constrained by our own education into trying to mould our thinking into getting the 'right answer', in trying to guess what a teacher wants and to give it to them in our responses. Young children have not yet had that experience of formal learning and therefore often do not respond in the way that you expect them to and that is fine, it is normal for them to express their creativity in that way.

ACTIVITY

It is sometimes difficult for us to step away from what we know and get in touch with our inner creativity. One way to develop this is to try to think 'outside the box', and to try to free our own thinking from what we know to what might be possible. Try this exercise, it helps to do this with a friend as you can share ideas.

How many ways can you think of to use a brick? Write down all of your initial thoughts and then share ideas.

Now think about changing the properties of the brick, what if it was larger or smaller, or made of different material?

Compare your ideas again and see if you can define what is your most creative use for a brick.

The wider curriculum

Because of the focus on the prime areas in the EYFS and the focus on the core subjects of Literacy and maths in Key Stage 1 the wider aspects of the curriculum such as Understanding the World, Expressive Arts and Design, History, Geography Science and Technology can often feel difficult to fit into the children's day.

It is also important to remember that for some children learning to read, write and count is challenging. Writing is a skill that demands the knowledge of the letters needed, the spelling of the word and the physical act of holding a pencil and forming those letters. Children may often not see the purpose of writing either, particularly if they do not see adults writing in their everyday lives. How many of us use text, e-mail or messages rather than writing? If a child is finding writing challenging and not enjoying it then repetition of the same tasks in the same setting will only serve to make them less inclined to want to do it. Even if they can write they may not feel confident and be reluctant to do so unless it is self-directed and part of their own learning where they have the motivation to do this. A focus on the wider curriculum means that literacy and maths become integrated or embedded into other areas and thus are seen as purposeful and meaningful.

Science and Technology

Science and technology start within the EYFS framework (DfE, 2017) in the Understanding the World section.

> Understanding the world involves guiding children to make sense of their physical world and their community through opportunities to explore, observe and find out about people, places, technology and the environment.
>
> (DfE, 2017, p. 8)

Children will develop this knowledge through guidance from practitioners so it is very important that children are given as wide an experience as possible, both within the setting and on visits and trips to learn about different aspects of the environment. This can include things that might seem quite commonplace to adults such as using a bus or a train which many children may no longer experience within their families. The development of this knowledge will underpin the learning in Key Stage 1 when key facets of the biological and physical sciences are explored. Children need to have experience of both natural and built environments and this is where outdoor learning is key to ensuring that all children can have the sorts of experiences that only some may have within their families. You can learn so much from a walk through a woodland, splashing in a stream and sliding in mud and trying to replicate this indoors does not have the same effect at all.

The non-statutory guidance for the EYFS Development Matters (Early Education, 2012) gives specific ideas as to what should be covered within this area of learning and development. The section is divided into three parts: People and Communities, The World, and Technology. An example of one of the things that children are doing between the age of 30–50 months from 'People and Communities' is 'Knows some of the things that make them unique, and can talk about some of the similarities and differences in relation to friends or family' (Early Education, 2012, p. 38). When they reach Key Stage 1 two of the outcomes are that they should 'describe and compare the structure of a variety of common animals (fish, amphibians, reptiles, birds and mammals, including pets)' and 'identify, name, draw and label the basic parts of the human body and say which part of the body is associated with each sense' (DfE, 2013a, p. 8). By being able to talk about similarities between themselves and recognising the differences between them and their cat for example they will be able to achieve the outcomes expected as they will have had the opportunity to explore these things through a creative curriculum from an early age. The opening statement from the Science curriculum includes the expectation that 'pupils should be encouraged to recognise the power of rational explanation and develop a sense of excitement and curiosity about natural phenomena' (DfE, 2013a, p. 2). What better way to develop that excitement and curiosity from seeing first-hand the number of woodlice that live under a log or to see a rainbow in the sky?

Within 'The World' section an example from the same age range is 'Talks about why things happen and how things work' (Early Education, 2012, p. 40). In the Computing curriculum for Key Stage 1 children are expected to 'create and debug simple programs' (DfE, 2013b, p. 2). Children who have had the opportunity to observe cause and effect with a range of toys and resources will be able to produce logical explanations for why things happen and will be able to analyse the steps needed to create programs.

For the section on 'Technology', children aged 22–36 months should be showing interest in the following things: 'Operates mechanical toys, e.g. turns the knob on a wind-up toy or pulls back on a friction car' (Early Education, 2012, p. 41). The link between a creative curriculum in the early years and the National Curriculum can be very clearly seen from this opening statement from the Design and Technology curriculum: 'Using creativity and imagination, pupils design and make products that solve real and relevant problems within a variety of contexts, considering their own and others' needs, wants and values' (DfE, 2013c, p. 1). This is the creativity and imagination that comes from the chance to experience creative play and experiment with solving problems from an early age. One of the outcomes from this curriculum is that 'pupils should be taught to build structures, exploring how they can be made stronger, stiffer and more stable' (DfE, 2013c, p. 2). A child who has had the opportunity to build their own balancing course using loose parts such as planks and bricks will already have encountered this scenario and will not need to be taught these skills; they will already know how to do this.

ACTIVITY

Using the links in the references section familiarise yourself with the curricula for Science, Computing and Design Technology and explore the links between that and the three areas in Understanding the World in Development Matters.

Cross curricular learning and thematic learning

Cross curricular learning not only enables practitioners to cover more aspects of the curriculum in each session but also helps children make the links between them and involves them in learning which relates to them, linking back to one of the key themes of a creative curriculum being child centred. An example of this is in the use of thematic learning. Many of these plans start off with a key question that can then be explored by the children bringing in other areas of the curriculum.

An example of this would be the question 'why is light important?'

By discussing with the children, thus enabling them to be using their verbal communication skills, there may be a mention of the fact that at some points of the year we have less light than at other times. This links into the idea of seasons and the fact that the amount of sunlight in a day varies. Other children might be aware of facts such as too much sunlight can be harmful for you, using their experiences of when they have used sun cream in the summer. One very practical way to demonstrate why light is important is to experience darkness so the children could create an environment where it is very dark through for example building a den and comparing what they can and cannot see in the different environments.

To link in with the Science curriculum, you could look at what happens to a plant if it is not given light to grow; this can be done easily by planting some seeds in cups and then storing some in a cupboard and others on a windowsill. Children will be amazed to see the difference in growth, especially if you can use different types of seeds as some react to lack of light better than others. This can also link in with outdoor learning particularly if you have an area of the setting that is shady where the children can investigate if different plants grow where there is less light or if children can look at what grows in different places in a woodland setting. Extensions of this for outdoor learning can be to grow plants in light and shade and compare them and to grow sunflowers who naturally turn towards the light and grow rapidly, offering chance for prediction as to how high they will grow and comparison of the different heights.

Another example would be to ask the question 'what do my parents/carers remember about their childhood?' Children are usually fascinated by the idea of their parents being young and a good starting point would be to ask for a photo if a parent/carer at the same age as their child is now. This can develop into questioning about family resemblances, clothing worn and where they grew up. This links into the Science as it looks at the ideas of human and animal variance and the influence of environment. Young children will be able to discuss hair, eye and skin colour and think about why they might resemble their parents/carers or not.

There are also links to the History and Geography subject areas of the curriculum by thinking about when the photo was taken, what year was it and where were they living. This can be differentiated depending on the age of the group that you are working with as young children will only have a developing understanding of these ideas. Some parents/carers may have moved to the UK at a later age which gives an opportunity to locate different countries on a world map, others may have grown up in different towns so could be identified on a UK map and others will have always lived in the same area, giving the opportunity to look at a local map and ask children to think about the differences between the different maps.

Observation and assessment within the EYFS and Key Stage 1

Observation is used by practitioners for both planning and assessment of learning and development. Observation is a key part of your role as a practitioner and as you gain more experience you will find yourself being able to observe children without them noticing what you are doing. Observation can take many different forms such as snapshot, spontaneous, narrative, spider's web, tracking, event sampling and target child (Barber and Paul-Smith, 2014), and each type has advantages and disadvantages in terms of the ease of carrying it out and the information that you gain from it. It is particularly important that each child is observed by their key person who is ultimately responsible for recording their progress and for liaising with parents; however all practitioners can contribute to observation information. Many settings now use apps such as Tapestry Learning Journal or commercially developed recording sheets such as the Early Excellence Assessment Tracker (EExAT) which link directly to aspects of the EYFS which make it easier for practitioners to link what they are seeing to where the child is in their development.

ACTIVITY

Think about how children's learning is recorded in your placement. Does the setting use any form of standard template for assessment or record using apps on iPads?

What is the value of using video and photo evidence to record progress as opposed to written evidence? How is this progress shared with parents and carers? How does this recording link with planning for day-to-day learning?

If you are working with very young children, particularly those new to a setting, an important reason for observation will be in passing on information to parents, both informally on a day-to-day basis and in the form of the 2 Year Progress Check. The culmination of the observations and assessment at the end of the EYFS is in the profile which seeks to describe the child's development against the 17 Early Learning Goals contained within the Early Years Outcomes guidance (DfE, 2013d). This information is used by the child's teachers when they move into Key Stage 1 at the end of Reception to inform planning. Observation and planning is different in Years 1 and 2 as with more children in a class and the move away from a key person approach there will be more of a focus on whole class planning; however this will also include planning for small group work as a key focus of learning in Year 1. Assessment of learning in Key Stage 1 is done by SATs tests undertaken at the end of Year 2 but as these only assess literacy and maths skills it is important that observation and recording of learning in wider curriculum areas is carried out so that a holistic picture of the child's development can be given to parents and to teachers in Key Stage 2.

The exemplification materials (DfE, 2014) which give examples of the Early Learning Goals are very useful tools in thinking about you might record the learning of the children you are working with and can also help to inform your own planning. For example, Early Learning Goal 13 People and Communities includes the following aims.

> Children talk about past and present events in their own lives and in the lives of family members. They know that other children don't always enjoy the same things, and are sensitive to this. They know about similarities and differences between themselves and others, and among families, communities and traditions.
>
> (DfE, 2014)

You have observed a 4-year-old child talking with other children about their plans for Christmas and one child is telling another that their grandmother is coming to stay with them for Christmas and that they will have a special meal on Christmas Eve. Another child is confused by this information and tells them that the special meal is on Christmas Day and you have to have turkey as part of the meal.

In many cultures such as Polish the main focus of the Christmas celebration is a meal on Christmas Eve rather than on Christmas Day and the meal which usually consists of 12 dishes contains fish dishes rather than meat. The Polish name for this celebration is Wigilia which means vigil or waiting and the celebration is about waiting for the birth of Jesus.

ACTIVITY

Plan a cross curricular activity for children around Christmas celebrations

Looking at the different aspects of the curriculum how could you plan an activity that looks at different aspects of the celebration?
Which areas of the curriculum could you cover and how?
How would you ensure that the children have chance to share their own experiences and include children who do not celebrate Christmas, so making sure that the activity is child centred and inclusive?
How will you include creativity for the children?

Here is another scenario.

You notice that only a few of the children at your nursery setting choose oranges as their snack rather than apples or pears. You would like to find out why this is and also encourage them to try oranges.

ACTIVITY

Think about a cross curricular activity that you could do to link science, maths, food and technology to encourage the children to explore the properties of the different fruits.

Activities that you could use could involve cutting the fruit and exploring the different aspects, for example seeds, segments etc.
How could the children record who likes which fruit?
What food related activities could you do with the different fruits?
How can you use technology to support their learning? Think about using it to record their findings as well as to find out more about the different fruits.
Which skills will you be developing?

Evaluating and extending your planning

When you first start planning activities you may be focusing solely on one aspect of the framework or curriculum; this is to be expected as there are many aspects to consider for each area. As you gain more experience and more confidence with the children, start thinking about including more elements. A key part of this is observing what kind of things the children enjoy doing and linking that to the original topic. Listen to the questions that they ask about the world around them and then link different areas of learning into these.

For example, a child may ask you how old you are, or tell you how old their sister is. This could be turned into a question such as 'how do we tell how old someone is?' This can then involve all sorts of cross curricular themes such as looking at height as a measure of age; this links in maths and some opportunity for measuring and recording by using charts or photos, particularly if this is developed throughout the year with regular photos taken against a height chart so that the children can see how they develop. This may be something that they are familiar with from home and can be supported by them bringing in pictures of themselves when they were younger and comparing what they looked like at 1, 2, 3 years old etc. This will naturally lead on to questions such as 'do we keep on growing?' or 'are all 4 years olds the same size?', 'is there a difference between boys and girls?' These questions are all linked to both the Science curriculum but also to the child's understanding of the world and of their own families. You may have children that maintain that Daddies are always taller than Mummies and you can try and explore this with them as well.

Recording learning can involve written skills but should also involve the use of digital photography and art, a creative curriculum should always allow children many options in the way that they wish to display their conclusions, some will want to draw and paint pictures of their families, others may be very interested in the numbers involved in measuring and want to make a height and age chart.

Conclusion

Looking back at the central themes for a creative curriculum it is important to remember that the starting point should be the child and their natural curiosity about the world around them. This needs to supported by access to play opportunities that allow them to play with resources that encourage rather than limit their imaginations. Creativity is not just about art and music, it is about thinking of different ways to do things and exploring. It is about saying 'what happens if I do this?' and 'can this be done a different way?' It is about seeing the world as a place full of things that are linked to each other rather than divided up into lessons. A creative practitioner is one who watches, who listens and who remembers the wonder of new experiences and gives every opportunity for the children in their care to experience that by giving them time to develop their skills, to consolidate their learning and to build a lifelong enthusiasm for exploration.

References

Barber, J. and Paul-Smith, S. (2014) *Early years observation and planning in practice: a practical guide for observation and planning in the EYFS.* 1st edn. Luton, Bedfordshire: Mark Allen Group.

Bruce, T. (2011) *Learning through play.* 2nd edn. London: Hodder Education.

Burgess, T. (2007) *Lifting the lid on the creative curriculum NCSL.* Available at: http://dera.ioe.ac.uk/7340/1/download%3Fid%3D17281%26filename%3Dlifting-the-lid-on-the-creative-curriculum-full-report.pdf (accessed 25 February 2018).

Casey, T. and Robertson, J. (2016) *Loose parts play.* Edinburgh: Inspiring Scotland. Available at www.playscotland.org/wp-content/uploads/loose-parts-play-toolkit.pdf (accessed 25 February 2018).

Daly, L. and Beloglovsky, M. (2015) *Loose parts: inspiring play in young children.* St Paul: Redleaf Press.

DfE (2013a) *Science programmes of study – Key Stages 1 and 2.* Available at: www.gov.uk/government/uploads/system/uploads/attachment_data/file/425618/PRIMARY_national_curriculum_-_Science.pdf (accessed 25 February 2018).

DfE (2013b) Computing programmes of study – Key Stages 1 and 2. Available at: www.gov.uk/government/uploads/system/uploads/attachment_data/file/239033/PRIMARY_national_curriculum_-_Computing.pdf (accessed 25 February 2018).

DfE (2013c) *Design and technology programmes of study – Key Stages 1 and 2.* Available at: www.gov.uk/government/uploads/system/uploads/attachment_data/file/239041/PRIMARY_national_curriculum_-_Design_and_technology.pdf (accessed 25 February 2018).

DfE (2013d) *Early years outcomes.* Available at: www.foundationyears.org.uk/files/2012/03/Early_Years_Outcomes.pdf (accessed 25 February 2018).

DfE (2014) *Early Learning Goals exemplification materials.* Available at: www.gov.uk/government/publications/eyfs-profile-exemplification-materials (accessed 25 February 2018).

DfE (2016) *National curriculum.* Available at: www.gov.uk/government/publications/national-curriculum-in-england-framework-for-key-stages-1-to-4 (accessed 25 February 2018).

DfE (2017) *Early years foundation stage statutory framework.* Available at: www.gov.uk/government/uploads/system/uploads/attachment_data/file/596629/EYFS_STATUTORY_FRAMEWORK_2017.pdf (accessed 25 February 2018).

Early Education (2012) Development Matters in the EYFS. Available at: www.foundationyears.org.uk/wp-content/uploads/2012/03/Development-Matters-FINAL-PRINT-AMENDED.pdf (accessed 25 February 2018).

Forest School Association (2017) *Home page.* Available at:www.forestschoolassociation.org/ (accessed 25 February 2018).

Kirkham, J. A. and Kidd, E. (2017) The effect of Steiner, Montessori, and national curriculum education upon children's pretence and creativity. *The Journal of Creative Behavior,* 51 (1), 20–34. 10.1002/jocb.83

Knight, S. (2011) *Risk and adventure in early years outdoor play: learning from Forest Schools.* 1st edn. London: Sage

Rose, J. (2009) *Independent review of the primary national curriculum: final report.* London: DCSF.
Available at: www.educationengland.org.uk/documents/pdfs/2009-IRPC-final-report.pdf (accessed 25 February 2018).

Additional reading

Bruce, T. (2015) Early childhood education. 5th edn. London: Hodder Education.

Dolya, G. (2010) *Vygotsky in action in the early years: the 'key to learning' curriculum.* London: Routledge.

Knight, S. (2013) *Forest School and outdoor learning in the early years.* 2nd edn. London: SAGE Publications.

Knight, S. (2016) *Forest School in practice.* Los Angeles: SAGE.

Riley, J. (2006) Language and literacy 3–7: creative approaches to teaching. London: SAGE Publications Ltd.

Useful resources

Assessment and observation

Early Excellence Assessment Tracker – information and examples available at: http://earlyexcellence.com/eexat/
Tapestry Learning Journal: more information available at https://tapestry.info/

Outdoor learning links

Forest Schools: www.forestschoolassociation.org/
Creative Star – a useful site containing a number of suggested activities including those specifically for maths and Literacy from the links below:
http://creativestarlearning.co.uk/c/literacy-outdoors/
http://creativestarlearning.co.uk/c/maths-outdoors/
Loose Parts Play Toolkit – lots of useful practical ideas for setting up loose parts play: www.playscotland.org/wp-content/uploads/loose-parts-play-toolkit.pdf

Creative curriculum examples

Thematic ideas for history – www.keystagehistory.co.uk/keystage-1/outstanding-lessons/reception-topics/
Themed activities – this is a US site so be aware of differences in spellings but some good ideas for cross curricular learning: www.giftofcuriosity.com/thematic-units/
The Wider Curriculum – an example for Key Stage 1: http://caedmonprimaryschool.co.uk/wp-content/uploads/2016/10/Wider-Curriculum.pdf

Chapter 8

Communication and language

Jo McEvoy

CHAPTER AIMS

By the end of this chapter you will be able to:

- briefly summarise how children develop communication and language skills
- explain why the development of communication and language is fundamental to children's social, emotional and cognitive outcomes
- identify practical ways to support and promote communication and language in your setting
- critically reflect on how communication and language help to secure firm foundations for future learning, health and wellbeing.

Introduction

Take a minute to imagine what it would be like if you were not able to communicate your needs, feelings, thoughts or intentions to other people. Feelings of fear, loneliness and frustration may come to mind. Fortunately, the vast majority of you will not have experienced this because you will have used non-verbal forms of communication such as gestures, signing or written language to make yourselves understood. However, in order to process your thoughts you will have utilised your knowledge and understanding of language. Communication and language are inextricably linked. Babies are born with an innate ability to communicate (Murray and Andrews, 2000), despite not having the language through which to express themselves. Being able to understand and promote communication and language in your everyday practice has potential to make a lifelong positive impact on every child you support.

This chapter covers four key areas of communication and language:

- Communication and language as foundations for learning
- The development of communication, speech and language
- Theories of language acquisition
- Supporting language and communication in practice.

Communication and language as foundations for learning

Communication and language are vital for development and learning. Children with poor speech and language skills are at risk of poor outcomes in relation to academic achievement, social fulfilment and future employment (Law, Charlton and Asmussen, 2017). Conversely, those children with good early language skills achieve the highest in primary school in English and Maths (Snowling et al. 2011). Yet, a recent report commissioned by the Communication Trust (Gascoigne and Gross, 2017) identified a growing trend of under identification of children with speech, language and communication needs (SLCN) across education and health services, meaning that these children are not given timely support to catch up with their peers.

What is equally disappointing is that there has been a strong policy drive in the last decade to tackle the negative impact of poor communication and language skills on life outcomes. Following the Bercow (2008) review of services for children with speech, language and communication needs a number of policy initiatives were implemented. These included: the establishment of a national charity, 'The Communication Trust', the appointment of a Communication Champion for England and Wales, the commissioning of research through the 'Better Communication Research Programme' (Lindsay, Dockrell and Roulstone, 2012) and the provision of free nursery care and education for 2-year-olds in areas of disadvantage.

In 2015, the Communication Council reported that over 50% of children in some areas of disadvantage were starting school with poor speech, language and communication skills. The gap between these children and those in more affluent areas is stark. Evidence shows that by the age of three, children living in the lowest income bracket are already 17.4 months behind their peers living in the highest income bracket (Save the Children, 2014). Without early identification and intervention before the age of five, these children have an increased risk of mental health problems and lower levels of employment when they reach their mid-thirties (Law et al. 2017).

It is estimated that 10% of children have some form of speech, language and communication need (Communication Trust, 2011). Their difficulties fall into two categories of need, described as 'persistent' and 'transient'. A child with a persistent SLCN may have a physical impairment or long term learning difficulty, such as a speech or hearing impairment or a specific learning difficulty that includes language/understanding delay. These children will require the specialist support of health and education professionals. A child with a transient SLCN may have a short term difficulty such as a temporary loss of hearing, or 'impoverished' speech characterised by a lack of vocabulary, difficulty in understanding language, poor listening and attention skills or poor articulation. These children may also need specialist professional support, but it is likely that their need is temporary. With early identification and appropriate intervention, children with transient difficulties can be supported to catch up with their peers and reach their developmental milestones. Unfortunately, it is the children from poorer backgrounds who are more likely to experience transient SLCN. Given the critical impact of communication and language on future achievement and mental well-being, it is essential that you act as champions in promoting communication and language in your own practice and beyond. A good starting point is for you to consider the meaning of the three words; speech, language and communication:

- **Speech** involves using our voices to make sounds for talking. We use intonation, clear articulation and fluency to ensure the sounds we make are understood by others. An example of a child starting to use speech is early babbling or saying a consonant sound for a common word e.g. C for 'cup'.
- **Language** is a complex system of communication using a combination of words to express meaning. It involves following rules for structure and style. Children develop receptive language (understanding) before expressive language (speaking). An example of a child starting to use language is 'my go park'.
- **Communication** is how we share information through different means e.g. speaking, signing, writing, movement. It involves interacting with others, using verbal and non-verbal cues and following conversation rules. An example of a baby using communication is waving goodbye or pointing to an object and uttering a sound.

THINKING ACTIVITY

Communication and language skills support four specific areas of life:

- Learning
- Behaviour
- Social development
- Emotional development.

Can you think of an example of how communication and language skills support each of these areas?

Learning

Learning is an interactive process that involves the use of language, since it involves listening, asking questions, discussing and using language for thinking. For children, being able to articulate their thoughts and explore them with others enables them to extend their learning and opens up new possibilities. Language is also a prerequisite for literacy. Being able to read can open up access to an abundance of information, literature and knowledge and being able to write enables us to record and share new ideas, concepts and knowledge. When you consider how you support or teach young children, you realise that learning is very reliant on speech, language and communication in its many different forms.

Behaviour

Children need language in order to understand the expected norms and consequences of behaviour. Studies show that early language ability at age two predicts later emotional and behavioural ability (Clegg et al., 2015). This is because being able to discuss and articulate feelings, opinions and emotions helps children to get along with others. They are able to understand the consequences of their actions and make informed choices about how to behave. Children with refined language skills are less likely to experience frequent episodes of frustration and anger at not being understood by others. Therefore, they are less likely to display unwanted behaviour and more likely to exercise self-control, dealing with conflict through language and socially accepted forms of communication.

Social development

The early years are a critical period for the development of social and communication competencies. Studies demonstrate that children who do not achieve minimal social competence by the age of five and a half to six and a half are at risk of poor outcomes for the rest of their lives (Katz and McClellan, 1997). This is a result of the recursive cycle that enables a child to experience positive or negative responses to their attempts at interacting with peers. It is a process through which the child's pattern of social behaviour triggers a reaction from other people. A child who demonstrates unfriendly behaviour towards others may be avoided and experience feelings of isolation; whereas a child who is friendly towards peers is likely to be received with friendliness in return and gain social fulfilment. For children with delayed language it is difficult to engage in conversations and form peer relations. It is not surprising therefore, that 40% of children with language difficulties struggle to make friends (Durkin and Conti-Ramsden, 2007).

Emotional development

Young children usually express their emotions in physical ways. For example, frustration can lead to tantrums and excitement may be expressed through running around or laughing uncontrollably. Most children will begin to use simple vocabulary to describe emotions by the age of two. As they get older, with support and typical language development, they will start to use more vocabulary and complex sentences to explain their feelings. They develop empathy, which leads to integration with peers and better self-esteem. In 2016 a report by Public Health England on children and young people's mental health (PHE, 2016) identified communication difficulties as one of the risk factors for poor mental health. So great is the impact of communication on social and emotional development that speech, language and communication skills are now recognised as a national indicator for children's mental health and well-being (Law et al. 2017).

Thus, there is significant evidence to suggest that having good language and communication skills is a protective factor for young children against poor outcomes in relation to academic achievement and fulfilment in all aspects of life. As an advanced practitioner it is important for you to understand how children develop communication and language skills, so that you can lead practice, supporting parents and carers to promote language and communication with their children.

The development of communication, speech and language

Communication and language – a prime area of learning and development in the EYFS

There are three prime areas of learning and development in the EYFS; personal, social, emotional development (P.S.E.D.), physical development (P.D.) and communication and language (C.+L.). These three areas are interdependent and intrinsically linked. Therefore, we should not consider the development of children's language and communication skills in isolation, but take into account also their personal, social and emotional development and their physical abilities, which all contribute to being able to communicate effectively.

Early communication

Babies are expert communicators from birth; able to gain attention and responses from adults, they actively seek interaction with others. Gopnik et al.'s (2001) research into how babies think and communicate found that they responded to their parent's or carer's communication cues in much the same way as the parents did to theirs; by looking, listening and tuning in. These communicative actions all contribute to the baby's social and physical development. Babies quickly tune into sound; they are already able to hear in the womb. They respond to all noises, but appear to prefer human voices to other sounds and quickly learn to recognise the voice of their main carer. Physical actions also contribute to the development of language and communication. Specifically, these involve looking and making movements. Babies are fascinated by faces and spend time gazing into the eyes of their parents or carers and reaching out to touch them. They begin to imitate tongue and mouth movements and will frequently stop sucking during feeding to pause and look into their parent's eyes, before continuing the feed. These examples of social interaction and physical actions typify how social and physical development are interwoven within the development of communication and language.

Protoconversations

Remarkably, within two months of being born most babies begin to engage in conversation-like behaviours, described by Trevarthen and Aitkin (2001, p. 4) as 'protoconversations'. These are exchanges made between the baby and the mother (or main carer) which take on the form of a conversation, using turn taking, gestures, sounds, movements and words (from the adult), despite the baby not yet understanding language. A good example of this is the recent 'conversation' I observed taking place between my 5-month-old grandson and his mum.

Case study

Baby's conversation with his mum

My grandson initiated the conversation whilst I was talking to his mum. As he lay on his back and noticed our attention was not on him, he threw out his arms and jerked his body upwards using his feet to push up on the floor. He was frowning, eyes fixed on his mum and uttered a loud grunt each time he thrust his body upwards. His mother's reaction was instant and unconscious. Whilst continuing to speak to me, she moved her eyes to make contact with him and smiled, saying 'oh dear, is nobody talking to you?' She spoke in a high pitched voice, with an exaggerated expression and soothing tone. My grandson immediately stopped moving and his frown changed into a smile as he uttered a gentle

(*Continued*)

'aahhh' sound. This interaction took barely 5 seconds. His mum turned back to me and continued our conversation. Immediately, my grandson reacted in the same way as before and succeeded in gaining our attention again. This time our conversation stopped and we moved into a three-way interaction in which my grandson became the focus of our attention. His noises, movements, pauses and smiles were matched by our responses of words, pauses, smiles and tickles.

What I found most interesting about this interaction was the ability of such a young baby to lead the 'conversation'. His pauses indicated to us when it was our turn to respond as did our pauses for him whilst we waited for the reward of his cute smiles and baby utterances. It is also interesting to note that babies have the uncanny ability to be able to end a 'conversation' when it suits them. My grandson is quite capable of dropping his gaze or moving his head to face in another direction when he has had enough of communicating with us and no amount of coaxing will re- engage him until he is good and ready.

Developing speech sounds

As they develop their social, physical and communication abilities babies gradually begin to acquire speech and language. Early speech sounds are practised and developed through babbling. Babies hear and imitate the particular sound patterns of their home language. Babbling supports their physical development of tongue and mouth movements needed for clear articulation of words. It also supports the baby to start to use his/her own form of language, whereby a particular sound may mean a particular word e.g. 'ba' for bath. At 15 months most babies are beginning to use a few words consistently for the same objects, although the meaning may not be the same each time they use the word. For example, a baby saying 'cup' may mean 'I want a drink,' or 'Where is my cup?' or 'That's mummy's cup'.

Moving on to language

The next stage of development involves using two or three word sentences e.g. 'mummy gone', 'my do it'. Young children begin to use language to convey meaning and thought. When this happens children are unconsciously starting to apply some complex concepts. They are recalling images in their mind, translating these into words, or combinations of words and remembering which patterns of sounds make up each word. They use their voices to articulate these sounds, often with gestures and expressions to ensure their meaning is understood. Amazingly, they are unknowingly using some important facets of grammar: phonology, syntax and semantics.

- **Phonology** – when they are putting patterns of sounds together to form words.
- **Syntax** – when they select words and organise them to convey meaning.
- **Semantics** – when they make logical choices of vocabulary and phrases to represent the images in their mind and express their thoughts.

By the age of three most children are speaking in longer sentences, they talk out loud to themselves whilst playing and express their thoughts through language.

ACTIVITY

Without looking back on what you have just read, can you summarise the stages
that babies and children go through to develop communication and language?
Use these prompts to help you.

- Early communication
- Protoconversations
- Developing speech sounds
- Moving on to language

Inclusion

It is important to remember that not all children develop and learn in the same way
(DfE, 2017, p. 6). Children present with particular speech, language and communication needs (SLCN) for a variety of reasons that require us to adapt how we communicate with them. Some possible causes for children developing a SLCN are:

- ear infections – if a child has many ear infections, they may be unable to hear
  words, or hear distorted sounds, or find it confusing and tiring to focus on verbal
  communication
- specific difficulties in using their oral muscles effectively, which may affect their
  speech – for example, if a child has cerebral palsy
- difficulties that are passed down through families
- problems during pregnancy or birth that affect children's developing brains and
  contribute to their speech and language difficulties as part of a wider developmental delay
- a recognised syndrome or disorder that causes communication difficulties
- a lack of stimulation and support to provide the rich language experiences necessary to develop their speech, language and communication skills.

(National Strategies, 2008, p. 9)

Although some children may need alternative or augmented communication systems
such as electronic aids or sign language to support their communication, most children
will simply need you to make minor adjustments to how you communicate with them.
For example, gaining their attention before you speak, ensuring they are facing you so
that they can see your lip movements and interpret your facial expressions, speaking in
simple sentences, using gestures as you speak and reducing background noise.

Theories of language acquisition

Two opposing theories of language acquisition revolve around the nature/nurture debate. Are we predisposed to learn language because our brain is programmed to do
so? Or, are we reliant also on the influence of a language rich environment for the
successful acquisition of language? Most theorists accept that it is a combination of
the two, but emphasise either nature or nurture.

Nativist theory

Noam Chomsky (1957, 1965, cited in Head, 2013) believed that children are born with an innate ability to acquire and learn the languages to which they are exposed. He proposed that the brain is wired to automatically make sense of the nuances of grammar and linguistic rules of language; meaning that children can instinctively start to recognise and imitate the sound patterns they hear, develop vocabulary and form sentences. He called this ability their Language Acquisition Device (LAD). Chomsky noted that children manage to form grammatically correct or grammatically plausible language structures even if these are not modelled to them correctly. Not all children are brought up in a family that uses grammatically correct language structures when speaking, yet they manage to make sense of language and use plausible language rules which appear to be logical, based on established rules for grammar. For example, they often make up their own version of the past tense for a verb: 'I sleeped at nana's house'. Although 'sleeped' is in fact an incorrect version of the past tense for this verb, it makes sense to use it, based on the premise that most past tense verbs end in 'ed'.

Interactionist theory

Vygotsky (1962, cited in Doherty and Hughes, 2014) proposed that children acquire language through social interaction within their cultural environment. Based on his learning theory of socio-constructivism, which involves the co-construction of knowledge with others; Vygotsky believed that children developed their linguistic skills as a result of their inner motivation to be understood by others, which is driven by an in – built need for human contact and interaction. Bruner (1983, cited in Doherty and Hughes, 2014) built on this theory and suggested that the interactions that children had with adults were significant because they provided support to develop and extend their language and make sense of it. He described this as the Language Acquisition Support System (LASS). Vygotsky also emphasised the link between language and thinking. He believed these were merged into one, because children use internal dialogue to represent, process and understand their thoughts and cognitive reasoning.

Cognitive theory

Piaget (1932, cited in Doherty and Hughes, 2014) believed that children learn independently through constructing knowledge for themselves, based on experience, experimentation, repetition and in accordance with their cognitive stage of development. For Piaget, the concept of object permanence was crucial to language acquisition. If a child understood that objects were still there when out of sight, that meant they had the ability to represent symbols in their minds, meaning that they could represent thoughts as words and translate words into language. Piaget's theory was similar to the nativist theory in that both viewed language acquisition as a natural process linked to prescribed stages of maturation.

Behaviourist theory

Behaviourists proposed that language acquisition was a learned behaviour that develops through a process of conditioning. They described two types of conditioning that stimulate the development of language (Brown, 2006):

- Classical conditioning involves the association of one event with another. For language development this equates to word association, in which the child begins to associate particular sounds, words or gestures with events or meaning. For example, the baby quickly learns that the request 'Wave bye bye' is associated with the imminent departure of another person. When that person happens to be the main caregiver the association with 'Wave bye bye' can cause the baby to become distressed.
- Operant conditioning is the process whereby the child learns through rewards or punishments. The baby who utters his/her first words is rewarded with smiles and praise. This prompts the baby to repeat the word and so the cycle continues and the baby's language develops. Conversely, a child who receives negative or infrequent response to their attempts at speaking is likely to give up trying and may potentially experience a language delay.

However, Bandura (1977) highlighted the social aspect of behavioural learning. Social learning theory suggests that children develop their language skills through repeated exposure to language in the home. Babies learn to talk through observing their caregivers, mirroring their facial movements and imitating their sounds. They notice how language is used during social interaction and start to copy this behaviour in order to initiate interactions of their own.

THINKING ACTIVITY

Which theory of language acquisition makes most sense to you?
    Can you describe an example from your practice to illustrate why you identify with this theory?

Supporting language and communication in practice

The EYFS (DfE, 2017, p. 6) emphasises the importance of learning through positive relationships and enabling environments. For children developing speech, language and communication skills this involves feeling securely attached to and valued by the adults who care for them and being motivated to use language by having genuine purposes for communication.

Positive relationships

Establishing positive relationships opens up the potential to support, facilitate and extend children's communication and language skills. By tuning into children's needs and interests you can help to create a safe environment in which spontaneous opportunities for speaking and communicating can be exploited.

For most children the home environment offers rich opportunities and motivators for language and communication. Conversations that children engage in at home can lead to 'sustained shared thinking' (Siraj-Blatchford et al., 2002), in which the two participants co- construct ideas and meanings, as they engage in dialogue that involves an exchange of thoughts and opinions.

Less flexible routines, staffing structures and time factors mean that it is not always easy to replicate in the setting language opportunities afforded to children through their home environments. However, there are a number of language facilitation techniques available for supporting children in your setting, including the following.

OWL

The OWL technique requires you to 'Observe, Wait and Listen'. When interacting with a baby you *observe* what has captured their interest (a ball) and instead of responding immediately, you *wait*. You might lean in and look expectantly at the ball and then at the child, then *listen*. After a pause, the baby will often respond through non- verbal communication; pointing or looking, but sometimes the baby may be prompted to utter a verbal response, for example, 'ba' for 'ball'.

The OWL strategy is also effective in helping children develop their speech by assimilating your language. For example, you may ask the child 'What would you like to do?' and then wait for a response. After a pause of 10 seconds or more, the child may respond by saying 'My play out'. During the 10 second pause the child had to process the question, think of the answer, compose the response and then speak it.

The OWL strategy reminds us that children need plenty of time to process language and then compose a response. Children develop receptive language (understanding) before they develop expressive language (speaking), so it is important to always allow them plenty of time to work out how to express their thoughts, rather than rushing in with a prompt or another question.

Follow the child's lead

A good way of motivating children to talk is to show them that you are interested and confident in their ability to take the lead. For babies or non-verbal children, it is important to try to show them that you want to understand what they are communicating. You might do this by mirroring their actions and joining in with their play. Imitating, interpreting and giving feedback builds up children's confidence and reinforces their motivation to initiate conversations when they have developed the language to do so. The strategy is equally important for children who are using spoken conversational language. Encouraging children to start conversations and following their lead shows that you are genuinely interested in what they have to say.

Provide language for children

We often ask questions of children when they do not have the vocabulary or language to be able to respond. When we do this we may miss opportunities to promote the child's language development and undermine the child's confidence. A common example is when a toddler shows us a new toy. We may respond by saying 'ooh, what is it?' The baby may not have the vocabulary to name it. Then our role is to *provide* language. Through modelling, narrating and speaking aloud our thoughts and actions we are providing a language rich environment and building up children's vocabulary. Research suggests that children need to hear a word approximately 14 times to be able to own it, remember it and use it themselves (Marzano, 2004).

Expansions

An expansion is when the adult repeats a phrase that the child says and then adds a little more to expand on it. For example, the child may say 'Up ... car up' and the adult may respond, saying 'The car is going up and up the hill'. The adult extends the child's language by providing new vocabulary and support for speaking in simple sentences. With older children who can already speak in simple sentences, the adult may use this strategy to introduce a new grammatical structure, or expand the sentence to add more information. For example, if the child says, 'I went to Hannah's party', the adult may reply, 'Yes, you went to Hannah's birthday party at the swimming baths.'

Open questions

When deciding on when and how to ask questions you will need to consider the child's stage of development. A child with limited vocabulary and language skills will gain more from you modelling language than asking questions. This is because they need to build up vocabulary and imitate language structures. However, for children who are using language confidently, they will benefit from questions that promote thinking and require them to compose answers using sentences. These are called 'open questions' because they leave open many options for how they can be answered. For example, 'Did you have a good time today?' is a closed question because the answer requires only a one-word answer, 'yes' or 'no'. However, when the question is asked as an open question, 'What did you enjoy about the party today?' it invites a more thoughtful response that requires the use of more advanced language skills.

ACTIVITY

1 Seek permission to observe a practitioner in your placement setting as they interact with children. Look out for examples of the practitioner using the language facilitation techniques listed above.
2 Ask the same practitioner to observe you and to note if you use any of the techniques.
3 Reflect on how you might develop your skills in facilitating children's use of language.

Enabling environments

As an advanced practitioner you should aim to create an environment that promotes communication and supports the development of language skills. A good way of doing this is to make an audit of your provision, considering the physical and the emotional environment. Your audit should identify 'communication enablers' and 'communication barriers'. Examples of communication enablers might be the areas or provision which prompt children to talk and engage in conversations (e.g. role play, books, small world) and routines or practice that promote language and communication (e.g. snack time, circle time, stories and rhyme). Barriers to communication may include overcrowded areas of provision that are too noisy, rushed activities or the team's lack of confidence in supporting communication and language. Once you have identified the enablers and barriers you can work with your team and the parents to develop an inclusive, communication enhancing environment. Some features of a communication enhancing environment include the following.

Visual symbols

Visual symbols are accessible to children across all the stages of language acquisition. They are particularly helpful for non-verbal children or those who do not understand English. A visually rich environment promotes inclusion. Consistency and continuity are paramount to the successful implementation of visual symbols but practitioners need to be aware that specialist services may use their own symbols for children with specific communication needs. Even so, simple outlines or photographs are very helpful for supporting children's understanding of routines, expectations for behaviour and the organisation of the environment.

Communication friendly spaces

Many settings have drawn on the work of Elizabeth Jarman (2007) to guide them in creating communication friendly spaces. These are quiet and contained spaces where two or three children can gather and chat alone or with adults. Often they are made from lengths of fabric draped over furniture to create a 'den' type area containing a few books, puppets or other suitable stimuli for talking.

Story telling

Children learn language through hearing stories. Stories are a great way of sharing language patterns, rhymes and vocabulary and language structures. Sharing stories without books supports children to tune into oral language, as they listen attentively to the storyteller and join in with repeated refrains and actions.

Dialogic book talk

Dialogic book talk involves a group activity where the adult and children develop a shared understanding of a book, through talking and chatting about it. Drawing on collaborative enquiry and using language for thinking, children are encouraged to make connections with their own experiences. The benefits of dialogic book talk are that it:

- acknowledges and extends children's experiences and develops their vocabulary
- develops children's oral language
- builds up vocabulary
- improves expressive language skills.

ACTIVITY

Make a list of the communication enablers and the communication barriers in your setting. What actions could you take to create a more communication enabling environment?

Conclusion

This chapter has provided you with a brief summary of how children acquire communication and language skills. It highlighted the importance of communication and language as a foundation for children's social, emotional and cognitive development. Practical strategies were offered to help you to promote children's communication and language development. As an advanced early years practitioner you will be in a position to act as a champion for communication and language in your setting and beyond. Try to spend some time reflecting upon your role as a potential champion for the development of children's speech, language and communication. Think about how you can ensure that best practice becomes common practice, so that all children are supported to reach their potential.

References

Bandura, A. (1977) *Social learning theory.* New York: General Learning Press.

Bercow, J. (2008) *The Bercow Report: a review of services for children and young people (0–19) with speech, language and communication needs.* Nottingham: DCSF.

Brown, H.D. (2006) *Principles of language learning and teaching.* 5th edn. Harlow: Pearson Longman.

Bruner, J.S. (1983) *Child's talk: learning to use language.* Oxford: Oxford University Press. Cited in J. Doherty and M. Hughes (2014) *Child development theory and practice 0–11.* 2nd edn. Harlow: Pearson Education.

Chomsky, N. (1957) *Syntactic structures.* The Hague: Mouton. Cited in C. Head, C. (2013) Communication and language. In I. Palaiologou (ed.) *The early years foundation stage: theory and practice* (pp. 366–380). Los Angeles: Sage.

Chomsky, N. (1965) *Aspects of the theory of syntax.* Cambridge, MA: MIT Press. Cited in C. Head, C. (2013) Communication and language. In I. Palaiologou (ed.) *The early years foundation stage: theory and practice* (pp. 366–380). Los Angeles: Sage.

Clegg, J., Law, J., Rush, R., Peters, T.J. and Roulstone, S. (2015) The contribution of early language development to children's emotional and behavioural functioning at 6 years: an analysis of data from the Children in Focus sample from the ALSPAC birth cohort. *Journal of Child Psychology and Psychiatry,* 56 (1), 67–75.

Communication Council (2015) *The links between children and young people's speech, language and communication needs and social disadvantage,* briefing paper. Available at: www.thecommunicationtrust.org.uk/media/381242/the_links_between_children_and_yp_s_slcn_and_social_disadvantage_final.pdf (accessed 19 February 2018).

Communication Trust (2011) *Let's talk about it: what new teachers need to know about communication skills.* London: Communication Trust.

Department for Education (DfE) (2017) *Statutory framework for the early years foundation stage (EYFS).* London: Crown Copyright.

Doherty, J. and Hughes, M. (2014) *Child development theory and practice 0–11.* 2nd edn. Harlow: Pearson Education.

Durkin, K. and Conti-Ramsden, G. (2007) Language, social behavior and the quality of friendships in adolescents with and without a history of specific language impairment. *Child Development,* 78 (5), 1441–1457.

Gascoigne, M. and Gross, J. (2017) *Talking about a generation.* London: The Communication Trust. Available at: www.thecommunicationtrust.org.uk/media/540327/tct_talkingabout ageneration_report_online.pdf (accessed 19 February 2018).

Gopnik, A., Meltzoff, A. and Kuhl, P. (Eds) (2001) *How babies think.* London: Weidenfeld and Nicholson.

Head, C. (2013) Communication and Language. In I. Palaiologou (ed.) *The early years foundation stage: theory and practice* (pp. 366–380). Los Angeles: Sage.

Jarman, E. (2007) *Communication friendly spaces. improving speaking and listening skills in early years foundation stage.* Nottingham: Basic Skills Agency.

Katz, L.G. and McClellan, D. (1997) *Fostering social competence in young children. the teacher's role.* Washington, DC: National Association for the Education of Young Children.

Law, J., Charlton, J. and Asmussen, K. (2017) *Language as a child wellbeing indicator.* London: Early Intervention Foundation.

Lindsay, G., Dockrell, J. and Roulstone, S. (2012) *Better communication research programme, improving provision for children and young people with speech, language and communication needs.* London: DfE.

Marzano, R. (2004). *Building background knowledge for academic achievement: research on what works in schools.* Alexandria, VA: ASCD.

Murray, L. and Andrews, L. (2000) *The social baby: understanding babies' communication from birth,* Richmond: UK CP Publishing.

National Strategies (2008) *The inclusion development programme supporting children with speech, language and communication needs: guidance for practitioners in the early years foundation stage.* Nottingham: DCSF Publications. Crown Copyright.

Piaget, J. (1932) *The moral judgement of the child.* New York: Macmillan. Cited in J. Doherty and M. Hughes (2014) *Child development theory and practice 0–11.* 2nd edn. Harlow: Pearson Education.

Public Health England (2016) *The mental health of children and young people in England.* London: PHE publications gateway number: 2016417 © Crown copyright 2016.

Save the Children (2014) *Read on. Get on: how reading can help children escape poverty.* London: Save the Children.

Siraj-Blatchford, I., Sylva, K., Muttock, S., Gilden, R. and Bell, D. (2002). *Researching effective pedagogy in the early years.* London: DfES.

Snowling, M. J., Hulme, C., Bailey, A. M., Stothard, S. and Lindsay, G. (2011) *Language and literacy attainment of pupils during early years and through KS2: does teacher assessment at five provide a valid measure of children's current and future educational attainments?* Department for Education research report. Available at: www.education.gov.uk/publica tions/eOrderingDownload/DFE-RR172a.pdf (accessed 23 February 2018).

Trevarthen, C. and Aitkin, K. J. (2001) Infant intersubjectivity: research, theory and clinical application. *Journal of Child Psychology and Child Psychiatry,* 42 (1), 3–43.

Vygotsky, L.S. (1962) *Thought and language.* Cambridge MA: MIT Press. Cited in J. Doherty and M. Hughes (2014) *Child development theory and practice 0–11.* 2nd edn. Harlow: Pearson Education.

Further reading

Hayes, C. (2016) *Language, literacy and communication in the early Years: a critical foundation.* Northwich: Critical Publishing Ltd.
Palmer, S. and Bayley, R. (2013) *Foundations for literacy; a balanced approach to language, listening and literacy skills in the early years.* 4th edn. London: Featherstone, Bloomsbury Publishing.

Websites

ICAN: www.ican.org.uk/
The Communication Trust: www.thecommunicationtrust.org.uk/

Chapter 9

Advanced academic skills and your major study

Lindsey Watson and Andrew Youde

CHAPTER AIMS

By the end of this chapter you will be able to:

- incorporate advanced academic skills into both assignment work and professional practice
- conduct a substantial piece of independent research
- understand how to write a coherent major study.

Introduction

The major study, or dissertation, synthesises all the skills, knowledge and understanding you have developed over the course of your degree into one significant piece of research. The knowledge and understanding you have gained will be around the early years curriculum and practice with a range of skills developed, including critical analysis, synthesis of ideas, original thinking, referencing, presentation and proof reading, all underpinned by a breadth and depth of reading. On completion of the degree, you will be bestowed graduate status by your university at a graduation ceremony. This act signifies that you are an independent learner, capable of taking on challenges presented in either employment or further study. In these contexts, problem solving and independent research skills are vital, as well as the ability to present your work in a variety of professional formats. It can be useful to see your major study as a stepping stone into employment or further study.

What is a major study?

There are three broad categories of early years major studies:

- empirical research
- literature-based research
- resource design, development and evaluation.

Empirical research

This approach involves the collection and analysis of primary data based on observations and experiences within early years contexts, for example, a setting or Forest School, or based on a group of children, or a particular child. Students obtain their own data to address a specific question or issue. This is the most common type of major study undertaken on early years courses, and this chapter largely focuses on this approach.

Literature-based research

This approach involves the collection, review and critical analysis of a range of secondary literature sources to address a specific question or issue. While all major studies will include a literature review (see the Literature Review section), it is possible to produce a piece of work that is entirely based on a review of literature. If you do this, it is important to review the literature from an explicit angle, and identify some themes to make the review distinctive. You might, for example, explore empirical early years research about your topic. Secondary sources are those written by someone else and include:

- academic literature
- theory
- early years practitioner periodicals, for example, *Nursery World*
- government policy and guidance.

Resource design, development and evaluation

An option becoming increasingly popular in early years major studies is the design, development and evaluation of an enterprise or resource. Examples of this approach include:

- proposing and developing an enterprise, for example, a business plan for a start-up nursery or parent/child group
- designing an educational 'app'
- designing an educational space, for example, an outdoor play area
- designing a short series of sessions for a particular group of children, for example, children who may have a specific additional need.

Whilst this is a more practical approach, it still needs to be underpinned by theory, academic literature and recognised good practice within the scope of the topic. For example, the design of an outdoor play area should be rooted in relevant theory (for example, theories of child development) and academic literature, with appropriate evaluation practices outlined, which could include observation and interviews. Hence, aspects of primary research outlined later in this chapter can still underpin this approach to major studies. Further, this approach can align with an Action Research methodology (see Methodologies section) where a change is made, such as the introduction of a new resource, and its impact is evaluated.

Critical reflection and critical analysis

At this advanced level of study, it is important that you can engage in critical reflection and analysis, skills which increasingly underpin your studies as you develop your academic writing and professional practice. The ability to take a critical stance on professional discussions, your own practice, the practice of others and observations of children impacts all your assignments and will be a crucial element to all aspects of your major study.

An important element of effective early years practice is critical reflection, which offers the opportunity to consider the impact of our actions on the children we work with, their families, colleagues and your own professionalism (Dyer and Firth, 2018). As an early years practitioner, you are required to move beyond description, adopting a critical stance on many aspects of early childhood education policies, initiatives and research and consider their influence on practice, moving beyond description (Papatheodoru and Wilson, 2016). One of the key ways that you will demonstrate your ability to be critically reflective is through the process of writing, which can often help you to understand things; as Bassot (2016) suggests, if you want to understand more about your own practice, you need to write about it. The act of writing encourages you to think about what you are writing, stimulating thought processes leading to the application of meaning. The process simulates the brain and provides focus leading to critical reflection (Bassot, 2016). It is important that you understand the expectations of critically reflective writing. A SWOT analysis (see Chapter 10) can help provide a structured reflection on the academic skills that you have developed throughout your degree studies.

To use 'I', or not to use 'I'; that is the question ...

It is always best to clarify the use of the first or third person with your tutor. Reflective writing is sometimes carried out in the first person, which can be difficult for those who prefer to write in the third person and proficiency in both is required when writing up within your major study. Using 'I, we, us, you' makes your writing more personable, as generally, critical reflective writing will include discussions around your own professional practice and opinions. As suggested by Dyer and Firth (2018), personal and or critical reflection can often include a level of discomfort often leading to a focus on negative analysis on aspects of practice; therefore, Bassot (2016) suggests being critical should be viewed as a critique potentially leading to a more balanced evaluation of practice rather than focusing on any negatives. Bassot (2016, p. 34) provides a good interpretation of what is and what is not critical reflective writing (Table 9.1).

The aim of reflective writing at this level of study is to move beyond the superficial, and promote questioning and challenges, key skills required in the data analysis of your major study. This requires effective critical reflection which needs to move beyond analysis of procedural roles, and facilitate conceptualised debate, demonstrating openness, flexibility and a willingness to view and evaluate situations from a range of different perspectives.

Linking theory to practice

An important element of critically reflective writing and critical analysis is the ability to support your own views and opinions using appropriate sources, situating your own opinions within the wider academic field. This typically involves immersing yourself

Table 9.1 What is, and what is not, critical reflective writing

Reflective writing is ...	*Reflective writing is not ...*
Written in the first person (I, we, you, us...)	Written in the third person (he, she it, they...)
Critical in the sense of offering a critique	Critical in the sense of it only focuses on the negative
Analytical	Descriptive
Spontaneous	Calculated
Free flowing	'Doctored' what I think I should write
Honest	'Kidding myself'
Subjective	Objective
About engaging with my feelings and processing them	A means of ignoring my feelings and burying them
A tool for helping me challenge my assumptions	An excuse to ignore my assumptions and allow them to influence my work in a negative way
An investment of time	A waste of time

within the literature (see Literature Review section below), helping to bridge the evaluation of your own opinions with those already recognised within the sector. Below is an extract taken from a student's major study, demonstrating effective reflective critical analysis that has drawn on the student's own data and the wider academic field.

EXAMPLE – CRITICAL REFLECTIVE ANALYSIS

Both adult and child participants valued opportunities to enjoy the freedom of the outdoors and the opportunities to manage risk however, in practice they experienced restrictions. Freedom to go outdoors was found to be restricted by external pressures experienced by participants.

> a lot of it is evidence in their books, on paper so I find that ... I think ...if I go out how am I going to provide that evidence.
>
> (Francine)

Curriculum issues present a barrier for Francine; she feels under pressure to provide evidence of learning in children's books. Francine values freedom of the outdoors (see values theme) but appears to experience a friction between these values and her practice as found by Waite (2011). Although other participants did not highlight this barrier, they discussed practice outdoors linked to curriculum areas. Furthermore, children's photographs (Appendix E) predominantly included break time activities, suggesting that lessons mainly take place indoors. These two factors indicate that demands of the curriculum take precedence over outdoor learning, an issue identified by MacQuarrie (2016). However, both Bilton (2010) and Waite (2010) argue the outdoors can allow holistic observation and therefore outdoor lessons could allow participants to identify new skills in their pupils.

This is a good example of how a student is critically reflecting and analysing on the findings from their major study, and including the voices of others to reinforce their opinions. Here the student has drawn on evidence previously discussed within the literature review to underpin and situate their findings within the academic field. Note the cautious tone adopted through the use of hedging words ('appears to' … 'suggesting that'), introducing the student's opinion whilst not over-claiming the findings.

Starting the major study

This section discusses practices and actions to establish a clear focus for the research. It firstly gives guidance on choosing a topic and developing a title, before moving onto to writing aims and/or research questions.

The major study will take a significant amount of time to effectively complete and, therefore, the most important consideration is choosing a topic that you will enjoy exploring further. Look back over your previous studies and see which you have found interesting and received good marks for. Also, reflect on your placement or work experiences and see if there are areas you would like to further explore. Do you prefer reading? If so, then a literature-based approach might be preferable. Alternatively, if you prefer something more practical, then an empirical or resource based major study might be more suitable.

Once a broad topic area has been decided consider the following questions to help you decide if the research is viable:

- Is the research within the scope of an early years degree?
- Is the topic worth researching, is there something to say?
- Is there literature/theory around the topic?
- Can you access a setting or children to obtain primary data? Will you be able to obtain permissions to conduct the research?
- Are there any ethical issues that may make the research too difficult to undertake? How would you explore poor parenting practices, for example?
- Are you motivated to research this topic?

A common mistake made by students is to choose a topic that is too big and unmanageable in the time allowed. It is better to undertake a small piece of research and explore it in depth – this allows more time for critical analysis and evaluation, which is key to getting higher marks. Empirical early years major studies are usually small-scale in broader research terms as they typically involve one setting and focus on a small number of practitioners and/or children.

Writing a title

The next step is to take a broad area of interest and develop it into a title. This requires an iterative process of reflection, reading and refinement to produce a title that outlines a clear focus for research. By thinking through the following stages (although not all will apply to all studies, literature-based approaches, for example), sufficient key words may emerge to help form a title, for example:

- Outline a broad area of interest – young children's play
- Develop this into a specific area of interest – risky play
- Specifically state the area of exploration – barriers to risk exposure in play
- Who is the research targeting? –children aged 4 to 7
- Where is the research based? – a primary school based in Yorkshire.

The following working title could then be developed – 'Exploring the barriers to physical risk exposure in play for children aged 4 to 7 in a Yorkshire primary school.'

Developing aims and research questions

Aims or research questions are developed to provide further structure and focus to major study research, and some studies include both. Aims express clearly and precisely what the study plans to achieve. They commonly start with active verbs, such as:

- to explore
- to investigate
- to examine
- to analyse.

More common in early years major studies is to set research questions. These form the core of the research, whether that be empirical, literature based or a resource development. A research question is a concise, clear, focused and answerable question around which your study develops. It is important to clarify that research questions are not interview questions (or questions that form part of any other method of research), although they are commonly the starting point for developing effective questions. Most importantly, they provide a strong reference point to ensure the research is focused and not drifting away from the original purpose. Research questions should be 'open', therefore, not answerable solely with a 'yes' or 'no', which forces the researcher to explore an issue in greater depth.

Literature review

The main purpose of the literature review is to:

- analyse what others have written about the subject, thus providing a breadth and depth of research around your chosen topic
- establish a theoretical framework for the study, thus providing academic rigour to the analysis of the study's findings.

This section of the major study synthesises the contextual literature that is drawn from textbooks, academic journals, early years periodicals and relevant reports. The treatment of these sources should be critical, analytical and creative; key ideas and themes need to be debated and contrasted, not simply listed and described. Try not to rely too heavily on specific sources or the discussion will not be balanced and you will be severely limited in your ability to provide a critical analysis. Synthesise the reference material where possible, often authors will be making the same or a similar point and these can be blended together. A poor style is when chunks of material are simply lifted from different sources and are linked together with a brief comment.

The literature review chapter should begin with an introductory paragraph that explains how it is structured and why. The review then provides understanding of a range of views, opinions and debates which can then be used to drive the research forward. For example, issues raised in the literature view can help when developing interview questions, questionnaires and observation schedules. This ensures the methods of data collection are providing feedback about a range of issues around a topic. The literature review can support the process of data analysis and writing up as the emerging primary data can be analysed in relation to the themes, issues and key findings generated from the reading. Further, the review can provide initial 'codes' that form part of the data analysis process (see Data Analysis section below).

Methodology

Within empirical major studies (and to a lesser extent in literature and resource development approaches) it is common to have a methodology section which addresses the following:

- justification of the chosen methodological approach
- justification of the chosen research methods and sample
- discussion of the steps taken to enhance your findings' validity
- ethical considerations taken during the research process
- justification of the chosen data analysis methods.

The chapter now moves on to consider each of these areas.

Research methodologies

The overall approach to research is called the methodology. Within the major study you need to identify and justify your chosen methodology; a good educational research book will help with this (see Further Reading and Research section below). A methodology is a system of methods used in a particular field, in this case education. In essence, it is the approach that is undertaken when researching an issue.

Whilst exploring the most appropriate methodological approach for your research, firstly consider the type of data that will be the most effective in answering the set research questions. Data or evidence to support decisions made when conducting early years research is commonly categorised as quantitative, qualitative or mixed methods:

- Quantitative data have a numerical basis, such as measures of improvement against EYFS criteria, and is adopted in larger scale research projects, such as a survey of the impact of a new phonics reading scheme across a number of settings.
- Qualitative data is more commonly used in small-scale early years research and explores meanings, experiences and opinions. Interviews and observations are key methods of collecting this data as they afford a deeper understanding of particular areas of practice.
- Research that elicits both quantitative and qualitative data is known as a mixed methods methodology.

Popular methodological approaches used in early years research are now outlined.

Action research (practitioner research)

This is described as 'to plan, act, observe, and reflect more carefully, and more rigorously that one usually does in everyday life' (Kemmis and McTaggart, 1992, p. 10). In an early years context, this refers to more systemic and rigorous reflection and research underpinning decisions made by a setting or individual practitioners. For example, a setting may want to introduce the idea of gender flexible pedagogy (Warin and Adriany, 2017) as part of their theoretical stance underpinning their practice. They would plan carefully how to introduce this by reading extensively around the area of gender. The practitioner may begin with visiting a setting that has already adopted the notion of gender flexible pedagogy. The setting then 'acts' by implementing this new aspect of practice, potentially carrying out observations of staff modelling of alternative forms of masculinities and femininities, the impact of a mixed gender workforce, and explicit gender pedagogy within curricula. Following a period of time, maybe a month, the practitioners within the setting will reflect on the new approach, drawing on the collected data, and then decide whether keep this approach and consider improvements going forward into the next Action Research cycle.

Case study research

This explores an instance in great depth to understand practice in a specific context with a view that findings may be generalised to other settings or groups of children. Examples of 'instances' in early years include a setting, a child, a practitioner and a Forest School. Therefore, a relevant example of early years case study research would be effective support for an EAL child within a mainstream reception class.

Ethnography

This, within early years, is the study of people and cultures within their natural setting. Essentially it is about time spent within early years contexts, 'hanging around' and understanding culture and practices. Participant observation is usually considered the main research method in this approach. It requires careful consideration when entering and leaving the setting in addition to how you position yourself as a researcher. Ethnography is both a process and product – so you would be expected to have extensive 'field' notes from the observations. Also, it is normal to write notes up immediately after observations have taken place.

Mosaic Approach

The Mosaic Approach uses a range of traditional and innovative approaches, including but not limited to narrative observations, interviews, photos, walking tours, children's drawings and emotion mapping, to gain young children's perspectives on their experiences in early years settings. Drawing on a range of methods, the aim is to facilitate knowledge production rather than knowledge gathering (Veale, 2005), giving younger children the space to step back, reflect and present their experiences, opinions and beliefs. This approach focuses on research *with* children, rather than research *on* children, giving children and other participants, such as parents or practitioners, their own voice rather than voicing opinions for them (Clark, 2010). The first stage includes wide-ranging data collection, before a second interpretative stage, which involves listening to the views of all participants, and valuing their input as co-constructors of knowledge (Roberts-Holmes, 2014).

Phenomenology

A phenomenological approach focuses on the ideas that, in order to understand some phenomena, such as the experiences of children, parents and practitioners, we have to view the experiences on their own terms. Thus allowing the phenomena to speak for themselves. This limits how much you allow your preconceptions or previous understandings to impact on this new, fuller or renewed understanding (Gray, 2018). Through inductive discovery, reflecting and modifying thinking, a phenomenological approach aims to interpret fragmented details of individual's experiences and perceptions, possibly gathered through semi-structured interviews and use this to create an interconnected view of the phenomenon (Smith et al., 2009). Phenomenological studies often include a small number of participants and focus on depth as opposed to breadth, such as using interpretation to gain further understanding of practitioners' perceptions of the use of digital technologies within early years settings.

Research methods

This section gives a short overview of common methods used to gather data in early years major studies. Within your major study it is important to justify why your chosen research methods were the most appropriate for your topic and research questions. This will largely depend on your choice of methodology and the type of data that is needed (commonly qualitative in early years research).

Questionnaires

These should be used when seeking broad information about a topic from a larger number of respondents, parental views of food options within a setting, for example. They are an effective means of collecting both quantitative and qualitative data, but are difficult to design and often require many rewrites before acceptable data is generated. A good questionnaire will include variety of types of questions and may include some open-ended questions. You should aim to receive a minimum of 20 questionnaires and, should this not be possible, you should look at alternative, qualitative methods of research, such as interviews.

Interviews

This method of research aligns with qualitative methodologies as interviews commonly unearth rich data about interviewee's opinions, perceptions and feelings about an issue. You can interview on a one-to-one basis or with a number of interviewees in a group. Most interviews fall into three categories:

- Structured – the interview is carefully thought out, questions are pre-determined and a plan of asking questions is followed.
- Semi-structured – the interview is focused by asking certain questions but with scope for the respondent to express him or herself at length or for the interviewee to prompt and ask follow up questions.
- Unstructured – in this type of interview, the interviewer may ask general questions but will then try to encourage the respondent to talk freely. The interviewer may well try to encourage the interviewee to give further information by probing and saying something like 'That's interesting, can you tell me more'.

Interviews are time consuming and this impacts on the number that can be undertaken. A common question supervisors are asked is 'how many interviews should I do?' For early years major studies, an approximate guide would be 10 short interviews that are roughly 10 minutes long, or 4 longer interviews, exploring an issue in some depth, that are over 30 minutes long. However, bear in mind getting a range of views about an issue (see the discussion of triangulation in the validity and reliability section), having sufficient data to argue credible findings and whether other methods of research are also being used as part of the overall research design.

Observations

There are different types of research observation methods and careful thought must be given to their choice. Firstly, you must be clear on what you wish to observe and why you think observation will provide the data you need. Participant observations involve the researcher participating in the daily life of a setting. However, the observer can change the dynamics of a situation, particularly if young children are involved. Alternatively, when the researcher does not participate with those being observed, this is known as non-participant observation. Both can provide a rich source of data but all from the researcher's own perception. They are ecologically valid, in that you are observing real life, as it happens. Observation can be used to determine whether people do what they say they are doing, or behave in the way they claim to behave.

Document analysis

A method of research that is growing in prominence within early years contexts is document analysis. Displays, pictures and writing can all be analysed to help ascertain children's perceptions of a topic. Further, a setting's policies, procedures and meeting records (minutes) can all be used as part of research into aspects of practice. For example, if a major study was exploring safeguarding in a setting, then a document analysis of the safeguarding policy would complement other research methods, and allow the researcher to evaluate whether the policy was effective in practice.

Ethics

Any research project must consider and address a number of ethical issues and questions. Sieber (1993, p. 14) defines ethics as 'the application of moral principles to prevent harming or wronging others, to promote the good, to be respectful and to be fair.' As an early years undergraduate student, you will draw on various professional bodies, such as the British Educational Research Association (BERA, 2018) and Ethical Code for Early Childhood Researchers (EECERA) (Bertram et al., 2015). These guidelines include an ethical respect for participants, knowledge, academic integrity and democratic values, related to designing an ethical research environment whilst also considering participant agency. Remaining consistent with an ethical approach, you will be asked to seek ethical approval from your institution before carrying out any research project. This protects you as the researcher, and anyone involved within your research.

Each major study is unique and will require you to consider an appropriate ethical approach, with this in mind, it is important that ethics are discussed thoroughly with your supervisor.

Positionality and reflexivity

As stated above, empirical research in early years major studies is commonly qualitative, and in this type of research it is the researcher who shapes the research design and analysis. If insufficient care is taken, this could lead to bias, whether consciously or subconsciously, on the part of the researcher. For example, if you are an advocate of free-flow play within nursery settings, you may explore this in your major study. You know six nursery managers who are also advocates of free-flow play and, as part of your research, you chose to interview them. Unsurprisingly, your major study conclusions, based on the interview data collected, will state that free-flow play is an effective method for young children's learning and development. The term 'Positionality' refers to the influence of the researcher's values and beliefs on their study and '..reflects the position that the researcher has chosen to adopt *within* a given research study' (Savin-Baden and Howell Major, 2013, p. 71). The researcher should consider their position in terms of their topic, the research participants and the research context (ibid, p. 71). Bias within an academic context can be defined as any influence that distorts the findings of a piece of research (Gray, 2018), and researchers should take steps to ensure the research is fair and balanced with findings underpinned with appropriate supporting evidence. To prevent this, a critical and rigorous understanding of ourselves, as researchers, is needed.

To foreground our values and beliefs and their impact on research, it is important for researchers to be reflective and reflexive. By being reflective, we can look back at our previous experiences and consider their impact on the research. Reflexivity is a more detailed examination of our values and beliefs in relation to a particular piece of research, with Dockett and Perry (2007, p. 51) describing it as a 'rigorous examination of one's personal and theoretical commitments'. By being reflective and reflexive, we make our position regarding the research explicit and the reader can bear this mind as they read your work.

When conducting research, steps should be taken to minimise the impact of the researcher's values and beliefs on all stages of the process. The following section discussing research validity outlines these steps and help you argue that your research is, as far as possible, balanced and fair.

Validity and reliability

This section outlines the steps you can take to conduct a fair and balanced piece of research by exploring the notion of validly and reliability in what are usually small-scale studies.

Validity gives an indication of how robust the research is and whether the topic was fully investigated; essentially, did you find out a true answer, as far as possible, to the issue explored? When we say 'as far possible' this because it is difficult to 'prove' in educational research as settings are complex, multifaceted environments with numerous influences on children's outcomes. When reporting researching findings, use of caution and hedging statements, for example 'the data suggest that' and 'this could indicate that', is commonly required. Actions that can be taken to enhance a study's validity include:

- Conducting a literature review, with breadth and depth, around the topic under investigation (see Literature Review section above).
- Choosing the right participants who, firstly, are knowledgeable about the topic area and secondly, represent a variety of views around the topic. A common approach in early years research is purposive sampling, where participants are selected for a clear purpose, usually because they have an in-depth knowledge of aspects of the topic under investigation.
- Piloting of research methods. It is important to test them to ensure the data being generated is addressing some of the study's aims or research questions. For example, you should ask two or three people to complete a questionnaire first before distributing it more widely to ensure the questions are clear, unambiguous and generating appropriate responses.
- Ensuring the research examines the same issue from different perspectives, or triangulation (Denscombe, 2003). For example, free-flow play could be researched by observations of children playing and interviewing the practitioner primarily involved in its delivery, this is known as 'triangulation by research method' as more than one method of research is being used to examine this issue. If both methods are unearthing the same findings, then the researcher can argue they have more valid data. Should there be discrepancies or inconsistencies in the findings, the researcher can explore why. Alternatively, both the children's and practitioner's perspectives could be explored regarding this new approach to play, this is known as 'triangulation by respondent' as two stakeholder groups' opinions are being sought about the issue. Again, if both practitioners and children are providing similar feedback, the researcher can argue they have more valid findings.
- Using a rigorous process of data analysis. This ensures that, as far as possible, the analysis of primary data is not influenced by the researcher's values, beliefs and potential prejudices about the area under investigation.

As stated above, early years major studies are usually small-scale. This makes reliability difficult to argue. Reliability considers whether the research findings would be similar if it was repeated again, or carried out within a similar setting, or with a similar group of children. If so, then you can argue the research is reliable and could be generalisable to other similar settings or groups of children. Early years settings are complex, multifaceted environments with numerous influences on children's outcomes and, therefore, it is difficult to generalise findings from one setting to another. For example, the other setting will have a different mix of genders, race, religions, socio-economic groupings and EAL children, which make up their cohorts. Therefore, key actions that a major study unearthed to improve practice in one setting may not be as effective in another.

Within empirical and resource development major studies you should include a discussion of the steps taken to enhance the research's validity. However, caution should be taken when arguing the reliability of research if small-scale. It may be prudent to argue that the research aims to explore a small issue in-depth within a particular cultural context of a setting, and therefore may not have generalisable findings. However, the findings may help similar settings with a largely similar group of children.

Qualitative data analysis

Qualitative data analysis commonly seeks to find themes occurring within the evidence collected. Unearthing these themes involves a systematic analysis of the data, such as outlined by Bryman (2016):

- Preliminary analysis, where notes are highlighted and significant issues are stated in margin notes.
- Breaking the data into incidents or issues – small chunks of information. Codes, or labels assigned to themes, are added.
- Systematic marking of the text with constant comparison of incidents and issues to establish themes, properties of themes, and relationships between themes.
- Comparison of identified themes from the primary data with the key themes outlined in the literature review.

This approach is commonly referred to as searching for patterns in the data. Patterns tend to hold meaning, and it is the researcher's job to analyse what they mean. However, sometimes inconsistencies hold meaning, for example, why are respondents' views polarised regarding a particular issue? Sometimes, a remarkable difference or instance is notable and worthy of further analysis.

Writing up

All major studies are unique. However, one similarity across every major study is that writing up will take longer than you anticipate; plan for this and make time available. Writing up requires you to present your findings in an engaging, coherent and objective manner, keeping it simple and accessible to a wide audience. You may think the logical approach is to write up your report after you have carried out your research. This is not necessarily the case, and the more time you can devote to writing up your different chapters whilst immersed within your research, the more the analysis process can help you to clarify your thoughts and keep the momentum going (Gray, 2018).

The title of the research should be concise, giving a sense of what the research is about, closely followed by an abstract of around 200 words, highlighting the aims, methods and findings from the research. This is usually written last. Many students add an acknowledgements section, appropriately thanking their participants and those who have supported them through the process, such as supervisors. Next, the introduction provides a rationale for the research, clearly explaining why it is worth reading, before leading on to the research aims/questions and the literature review. This is typically followed by the methodology, containing enough detail to allow the reader to replicate the study. An effective major study demonstrates interconnectedness between chapters, such as drawing on the literature review to support the discussion chapter. The findings and discussion chapters can be challenging due to this being a relatively new style of thinking and writing. Your academic skills throughout your degree have been preparing you for this, so anticipate the challenge and work with your supervisor on this chapter. Do not overlook the importance of the conclusion, as this is where you leave the reader finalising their views on your research. Henn, Weinstein and Foard (2013) illustrate six considerations of an effective conclusion:

- What were the main findings of the research?
- How do findings sit within the main context of theory?
- What are the implications of the research?
- What lessons can be learned from the experience of carrying out the research?
- What can be learned from the way the methods were employed?
- What areas are open for future research?

Reference as you go. This will probably be the largest and most in-depth piece of writing you have completed so far, so keep an up-to-date full reference list of all your sources and consider using an electronic referencing tool and storage system. There is often an appendices section within your major study, including examples of data collection methods and analysis, which will need to be clearly arranged to allow you to draw on the evidence within your writing up.

Conclusion

This chapter has provided an overview of advanced academic skills to strengthen your academic work and placement practice. It has also discussed theory and practice to support the completion of a substantial piece of independent research. The chapter included examples of students' academic writing and thinking activities to encourage you to reflect and develop your understanding of what it means to be critical.

Additional reading

Denscombe, M. (2017) *The good research guide for small research projects*. 6th edn. Buckingham: Open University Press.
Roberts-Holmes, G. (2014) *Doing your early years research project: a step-by-step guide*. 3rd edn. London: Sage Publications Ltd.

References

Bassot, B. (2016) *The reflective practice guide: an interdisciplinary approach to critical reflection*. Oxon: Routledge.

Bertram, T., Formoshino, J., Gray, C., Pascal, C. and Whalley, M. (2015) *EECERA ethical code for early childhood researchers*. Available at: www.eecera.org/custom/uploads/2016/07/EECERA-Ethical-Code.pdf (accessed 16 May 2018).

Bilton, H. (2010) *Outdoor learning in the early years*. Oxon: Routledge.

British Educational Research Association (2011) *Ethics and educational research*. Available at: www.bera.ac.uk/ethics-and-educational-research-2/ (accessed 16 May 2018).

Bryman, A. (2016) *Social research methods*. 5th edn. Oxford: Oxford University Press.

Clark, A. (2010) Young children as protagonists and the role of participatory, visual methods in engaging multiple perspectives. *American Journal of Community Psychology*, 46(1–2), 115–123.

Denscombe, M. (2003) *The good research guide for small research projects*. Buckingham: Open University Press.

Dockett, S. and Perry, B. (2007) Trusting children's accounts in research. *Journal of Early Childhood Research*, 5(1), 47–63. doi: 10.1177/1476718X07072152

Dyer, M. and Firth, N. (2018) Being a reflective practitioner. In McMahon, S. and dyer, M. (2018) *Work-based practice in the early years: a guide for students*. oxon: routledge.

Gray, D. (2018) *Doing research in the real world*. 4th edn. London: Sage Publications Ltd.

Henn, M., Weinstein, M. and Foard, N. (2013) *A critical introduction to social research*. 2nd edn. London: Sage Publications Ltd.

Kemmis, S. and McTaggart, R. (1992) *The action research planner*. 3rd edn. Geelong, Victoria: Deakin University Press.

MacQuarrie, S. (2016) Everyday teaching and outdoor learning: developing an integrated approach to support school-based provision. *Education 3–13*, 1–17. 10.1080/03004279.2016.1263968

Papatheodoru, T. and Wilson, M. (2016) The international perspective on early childhood education and care. In Palaiologou, I (Ed.), *The early years foundation stage: theory and practice* (pp. 73–89). London: Sage.

Roberts-Holmes, G. (2014) *Doing your early years research project: a step-by-step guide*. 3rd edn. London: Sage Publications Ltd.

Savin-Baden, M. and Howell Major, C. (2013) *Qualitative research: the essential guide to theory and practice*. Abingdon: Routledge.

Sieber, J. (1993) The ethics and politics of sensitive research. In Renzetti, C., Lee, C., Sikes, P., Measor, L. and Woods, P. (Eds), *Researching sensitive topics* (pp. 14–26). London: Sage.

Smith, J., Flowers, P. and Larkin, N. (2009) *Interpretative phenomenological analysis: theory method and research*. London: Sage Publications Ltd.

Veale, A. (2005) Creative methodologies in participatory research with children. In Greene, S. and Hogan, D (Eds), *Researching children's experience: approaches and methods* (pp. 253–272). London: Sage.

Waite, S. (2010) Losing our way? The downward path for outdoor learning for children aged 2–11 years. *Journal of Adventure Education and Outdoor Learning*, 10 (2), 111–126.

Waite, S. (2011) Teaching and learning outside the classroom: personal values, alternative pedagogies and standards. *Education, 3–13*, 39(1), 65–82. doi:10.1080/03004270903206141

Warin, J. and Adriany, V. (2017) Gender flexible pedagogy in early childhood education. *Journal of Gender Studies*, 26(4), 375–412. 10.1080/09589236.2015.105738

Chapter 10

Work-based practice

Your next steps

Samantha McMahon and Kate Aspin

CHAPTER AIMS

By the end of this chapter you will be able to:

- identify the skills, knowledge and experience you can exploit when applying for a job or postgraduate study
- write a personal statement
- understand the diverse routes into teaching and how to apply
- locate internet vacancy websites and additional careers advice and guidance.

Whilst many of our students on an early years/early childhood course know from the outset that they want to pursue a career in teaching young children, others are less certain and some final year students are still unsure about what they want to do after they graduate. Whatever stage you are at in thinking about what to do after you graduate, there is lots of help and advice available at university from careers advisors, tutors, postgraduate information sessions, and from visiting professionals at organised careers events. It is not intended that this chapter should replace any of this expert advice rather that it should complement it, and provide a useful starting point for students transitioning into their final year. As one student said, 'This is when it gets real'. Fortunately, because of the experience you have gained whilst on placement, you have a considerable advantage over students without this experience when it comes to applying for jobs and postgraduate teaching courses. As Ogilvie and Homan (2012) found in their research, students with experience in the workplace develop essential interpersonal, political and research skills, and they acquire organisational awareness. Their research suggests these are considered to be beneficial by employers and can have a positive impact on future employment opportunities for the student. The following section encourages you to reflect on the skills and knowledge you have accrued whilst on placement and at university.

Identifying your skills and knowledge

As part of your studies you have probably undertaken a SWOT analysis, reviewing your strengths, weaknesses, opportunities and threats. This can be a powerful tool to help you uncover essential skills and knowledge you can exploit when applying for a job or postgraduate study, and weaknesses which need to be managed.

To find your strengths you might start by writing down a list of your personal characteristics and values e.g. determined, conscientious, committed to inclusive practice, all of which are likely to be strengths. Then consider the following questions:

- What skills do you have?
- What specialist knowledge do you have?
- What do others say are your strengths?
- Which achievements are you most proud of?
- Which values and principles are most important to you?
- Which networks are you part of?

Importantly, once you have identified your strengths you can consider if they might open up **opportunities** for you. Then you might follow a similar process to identify your **weaknesses,** it is important to be very honest. You might start by answering the following questions:

- Are there any tasks you avoid because you do not feel confident doing them?
- Are you confident in your skills and knowledge, are there any gaps?
- What have others said are your weaknesses?
- Do you have any personality traits or characteristics which might hold you back, for example fear of public speaking?

Could any of these weaknesses lead to **threats**? (adapted from Mindtools Personal SWOT Analysis, 2018)

Up to this point you have approached the SWOT analysis from an internal or personal perspective; now consider it from an external perspective. To do this you could reflect on how changes in government policy might provide opportunities you can exploit, for example, the number of education and childcare places is expanding due to the government's plan to increase 'free 'provision. Is this an opportunity you can take advantage of?

THINKING ACTIVITY

Reflect on the following case study which includes elements of a student's SWOT analysis. Identify the key information the SWOT provided, some from an internal perspective, some from an external perspective, and the corresponding actions it prompted her to take.

Case study: Hannah

Towards the end of her second year of study Hannah completed a SWOT analysis as part of her professional portfolio (Table 10.1). After reviewing the report from her work based mentor, she identified that she worked well as part of a team and was extremely competent at assessing the children's learning, and planning accordingly. Hannah recognised these as strengths particularly as she hoped to apply for a postgraduate primary teaching course. However, as she continued to review her portfolio she realised that all of her experience had been in Reception. Whilst this meant that she had very good knowledge of the early years foundation stage (EYFS) it meant her experience of working with the National Curriculum (NC) was limited. Hannah identified that this might threaten the likely success of her postgraduate application. As Hannah had received a very positive report from her work based mentor at the end of her placement, she decided to contact her, and ask about returning to the school as a volunteer in Year 1. Her mentor was keen to support Hannah and helped secure this placement. The Year 1 teacher was impressed by Hannah's professional attitude and supported her in gaining invaluable knowledge and experience of working with the NC. Hannah continued to reflect on her skills and knowledge whilst volunteering in Year 1, and recognised that she needed to extend her understanding of how children learn to read and reading interventions, so she decided to make this the focus of her final research study.

Table 10.1 Hannah's SWOT

Strengths	Weaknesses
Team work	Lack of experience working in Years 1, 2, so limited knowledge of NC
Knowledge of EYFS	
Ability to assess children's learning	Little experience of teaching children to read (significant focus in Year 1 NC)
Ability to plan for children's learning	
Positive placement report, favourable feedback from mentor	Limited understanding of how children learn to read
Opportunities	**Threats**
Draw on knowledge and experience of EYFS for post grad application	Lack of experience/knowledge of NC could jeopardise post grad application for primary teaching (Years 3–7)
Contact placement mentor about time in Year 1/2 to learn more about NC	
Placement mentor to provide a positive reference on application	Lack of knowledge of how children learn to read, could jeopardise application/ interview for postgrad teaching
Identified topic for final year research study so can start research during summer holiday	

The SWOT analysis is one way to help you focus on your strengths and minimise your weaknesses, it provides a framework for you to audit your skills and plan your career.

In many countries employers complain that they cannot find workers with the skills they require, and at the same time graduates can struggle to find jobs that match their qualifications (OECD, 2017). If you have undertaken a skills audit and understand what employers are looking for, you have the opportunity for achieving a better alignment between the two.

What employers are looking for

There are a range of basic essential skills which most employers require, alongside specific knowledge or competencies. Employers will look for evidence of writing and reading skills in the application form, and presentation and communication skills at the interview. In addition, they expect you to be organised and that you can manage your time effectively. Increasingly, employers want to recruit candidates with resilience, that is the ability to overcome setbacks and work under pressure.

THINKING ACTIVITY

Stressful situations and things not going entirely to plan can be regular occurrences at work; employers want to know that you are aware of what you find stressful and that you can manage the stresses of work. Consider a time when you successfully handled a stressful situation, and identify the actions you took to mitigate the stress and the positive outcome achieved.

(adapted from Targetjobs, 2018)

Of course, qualifications matter but employers will often consider graduates with a degree in an unrelated subject, as they value other skills and characteristics such as confidence, collaboration, enthusiasm and a can-do attitude. They may want to see evidence of sustained involvement in a project or enterprise, for example, a work placement or extra-curricular activities.

Research into an organisation or specific job role will help you identify particular skills, knowledge, experience and qualifications required. Prospects (www.prospects. ac.uk) provide information, advice and job opportunities for graduates, and you can search an extensive range of job profiles which match your interests and skills.

THINKING ACTIVITY

Consider the following job profile for an Early Years Teacher (EYT) as set out on the Prospects website. Reflect on your skills, knowledge and experience; how do they align with this brief description? What evidence might you draw on to provide examples which demonstrate your suitability for this role? If you are interested in finding out about the responsibilities of an EYT and what qualifications and skills you require, visit www.prospects.ac.uk/job-profiles/ early-years-teacher

Job Profile EYT

If you think you've got what it takes to inspire, excite and nurture children through a crucial stage of their development, consider becoming an early years teacher (EYT).

As an EYT, you'll work with children aged 0–5 in various settings such as nurseries, pre-schools and reception classes. It's important that the activities you plan and carry out meet the requirements of the early years foundation stage (EYFS). Your aim is to motivate children and imaginatively use resources to help them learn. You'll provide a safe and secure environment for them to develop their social and communication skills, while recording observations and summarising their achievements. You should be focused on the development of the child to prepare them for a successful transition to primary school.

Tutors often provide references for students and employers and are asked to comment on the student's character, specifically their integrity, reliability and potential to lead. To do this they will consult with colleagues and records kept by the university for example, placement reports, tutorial logs and attendance registers. However, to write a reference which allows the student to stand out it can be very helpful to have additional insight into their life particularly if they have a talent, a part-time job or are involved in extracurricular activities at the university. We have been amazed to learn of the diverse range of talents and transferable skills the students have, for example teaching dance and drama, working as a photographer, playing semi-professional football and running an after-school club. With this type of knowledge, tutors are able to provide a more personal reference tailored to the student and the requirements of the job, or postgraduate course.

THINKING ACTIVITY

Consider the following case study and list any additional information you could share with your tutor when you ask them to provide a reference.

Case study

Sanna contacted me one year after graduation and explained that she had previously applied for a place on an MSc in Speech Therapy but had been unsuccessful. She was keen to try again and wondered if I would provide a reference. I agreed, and asked her if there was anything she felt I should know that would help her application. She explained that in addition to her part-time job as a teaching assistant, she had been shadowing a speech therapist for six months. Sanna spoke passionately about the work of the speech therapist, and I was able to include this in my reference, as it demonstrated her determination and commitment to the course and the profession. I was also able to comment positively on her resilience and problem solving skills as she bounced back from her earlier rejection and identified that she needed more relevant experience, and a better understanding of the role.

Towards the end of the chapter there is a list of internet vacancy sites which reflect the varied careers that students are interested in pursuing. Although many require further study it is important to be aware of the wide range of opportunities available, once you have achieved your degree including going on to work for the local authority, or going on to study play therapy, and social work. Advice from the careers service encourages students to be prepared to look beyond the familiar career pathways as there are opportunities in other sectors. One such sector is the police; increasingly officers have to work with vulnerable people and they are required to understand how disadvantage, domestic violence and mental health issues can impact on children and families. Therefore, the police service also need to recruit graduates with the specialist knowledge and skills to work with children and families. The following section provides some guidance on completing the required application form or personal statement. It is not possible to provide exhaustive guidance for every specific application form; however individual and personalised advice is available through the careers service at the university.

Completing an application form and personal statement

There are some key things which need to be considered when completing an application form and writing a personal statement:

- What message are you trying to get across in each paragraph?
- Evidence the skills, attributes, experience and knowledge for the job you are applying for.
- Ensure anything you include is relevant; do not include a story unless you outline what you learnt and how it is relevant. You might use the STAR approach, that is, outline the Situation and the Task, the Action taken and the Result.
- Make clear why you are interested in the job, is there a specific aspect of the role which interests you and why.

When completing a personal statement include:

- significant details from your degree, not necessarily every module but what you learnt, research projects undertaken, and relevant work experience including: age groups worked with, specialist skills acquired for example assessing children's progress, or teaching phonics
- key policy or legislation relevant to your developing understanding of practice for example relating to safeguarding or special educational needs
- other related skills or experiences for example from working on a summer camp, a part time job or from leisure pursuits such as art, music and sport.

In addition, always keep a copy, adhere to the stated word limit and be prepared to answer questions about your statement at interview. You can add impact to your personal statement by using positive action words, verbs, which make a stronger impression on the employer or admissions tutor.

A significant number of students who study early years related courses want to become teachers, either in early years or primary. The personal statement is a crucial

THINKING ACTIVITY

Consider the following statement, and identify the positive active words and the skills identified. What other key messages are conveyed in this statement?

> For my final year research project, I devised a questionnaire for parents and interviewed four teachers to gain insight into how children are supported as they transition into school. I analysed the data and presented the results to the staff, and the head teacher of the school. I achieved a 2:1 on this project.

part of the application process for a postgraduate teaching qualification and further information will be provided in the following section. It also presents information on the diverse routes into teaching and offers invaluable advice from the Postgraduate Initial Teacher Training Admissions Tutor.

Routes into teaching

This section will explore the routes into, and how to apply for, places on a teacher training postgraduate courses. By this stage of your degree you will have started to think about what to do when your course finishes. After placement experiences on your course, you may well have a very clear idea about where you want to go after you graduate (or even where you do not want to work!). If you have been on a full time three-year degree, you qualify for a further year of student loan which can cover Initial Teacher Training costs too.

Selecting a route

The range of routes into teaching have exploded in variety over the last few years and you may be a little confused as to which is the best route for you. They break down into several types:

1   University based qualifications: these tend to follow the traditional PGCE (Postgraduate Certificate in Education) with an attached QTS (Qualified Teacher Status) qualification, which have been running for many years. These usually involve two main school based placements and time spent in university in taught sessions.
2   School based qualifications (often known as School Direct or as SCITT courses): these are based at a school, with some taught sessions at a linked University. Some of these courses involve a PGCE, and some are QTS only courses. Some of these may have a salary attached, most do not. These often have two placements, following an A, B, A model where you attend one placement, and then do a short alternative, and then return to the first.
3   Assessment only routes: completed via a provider which could be a school or a university or a business like the Times Educational Group. These are suited to those with a great deal of school experience, and a teaching assistant position; most result in QTS only. These involve taught sessions, often via distance or blended learning. These usually involve working as an unqualified teacher (paid) while working towards your qualification.

4   Salaried routes: 'Teach First' is the best known of these; some School Direct routes have a salary attached. Newer apprenticeship routes will be coming on stream in the near future. Most result in a PGCE and QTS. These involve some face-to-face teaching, some blended and distance learning, often in holiday times to avoid eating into teaching time.

Case studies

Read through the following examples, and identify which training route/s would suit each candidate.

Husnah has graduated with a childhood studies degree, has some school experience from voluntary placements while in university and feels very comfortable in both school and university. Husnah has accommodation near university and does not drive.

Sam is a teaching assistant and has just completed an early years degree part time while working in school. Sam lives with her children and needs a route that will be paid. Sam does drive.

Richard wants to teach abroad. He has just graduated with a degree in education studies and has a range of school based experiences; he drives and feels comfortable in school or within university.

Which routes are the best for you?

A useful resource for information on ITT courses is the Department for Education Getting into Teaching Website (https://getintoteaching.education.gov.uk/explore-my-options), and local providers will hold open sessions advertised on social media to in-form would-be candidates about the routes that they offer. If you have any unusual qualifications or requirements (or special needs) it would be wise to contact your chosen providers to discuss these in advance.

Most ITT courses have to be applied for on the UCAS website (https://2018.teacher-training.apply.ucas.com/apply/student/login.do). The UCAS portal opens for applications in October prior to entry. It is wise to apply early in the recruitment cycle if you have a very specific route in mind, and unsurprisingly, routes with a salary attached tend to fill first. You may apply to three courses initially, and if you are unsuccessful, there is an opportunity to apply to more subsequently. UCAS has a blog site where applicants and trainees write about their experiences (www.ucas.com/connect/blogs/user/UCAS%20Teacher%20Training).

Personal statements

Having decided to apply for an ITT course and selected your three chosen courses, the next step is to write an effective personal statement. When you applied for your undergraduate course you had to write one of these and probably had some guidance from your school or college at that point. Writing an effective personal statement for a teacher training course is essential and needs to be tailored specifically towards the course. These are *all* read by admissions tutors and lead teachers for your chosen courses.

An effective statement will address why you want to do the course, and give some details of your experiences in schools or settings working with children. A wise idea is to remember how many applications the admission tutor or teacher will be reading, and consider how to make yours stand out from the crowd.

Avoid starting with an inspirational quote or saying how much you like working with children, instead imagine you are talking to a friend and explaining your reasons for choosing teaching. Highlight your experiences with children, and explain what you have learned as well as what you have done. For example, if you have supported a child with special needs, talk about what you have done, but also what it taught you about teaching in general. Wider aspects of your life also enhance a personal statement, so a part-time job in retail can be used to support your ability to work with the general public and link back to working with the wider public and parents and carers in teaching situations. If you have helped in youth groups, or with organisations such as Scouts or Rainbows try to make links across to teaching, so consider safeguarding aspects, conducting risk assessments etc. and write this into strengthen your statement.

You also need to ensure that your written English is of good quality and clarity. Find a 'critical friend' who can proofread for you and give you advice, check for formality of language and spelling, punctuation and grammar. If a head teacher or class teacher could read through your statement and suggest improvements this can be a huge help, after all they could well be your future employer!

The people reading your statement need to be convinced that teaching is your passion and that you have a good range of school or setting experience, so ensure you talk about the schools you have been in, what you did and learned while you were there. Avoid giving a total of hours spent in school; rather discuss year groups and activities completed instead. Do consider the year groups you have applied to teach in too. So if you apply to a 3–7 focused ITT course, you need to have had experience in EYFS and Key Stage 1; if you apply to a 5–11 course then experience in Key Stage 1 and 2 is wise and demonstrates commitment and a basic level of knowledge.

Check list for an effective personal statement

- Ensure details of school experience are a strong focus.
- Do mention all experiences with children: from babysitting to volunteering work with groups like Rainbows and Cubs.
- Do not waste words on quotes or saying you like children.
- Do make links to showcase your knowledge of key topics. For example – 'My regular commitment to the local Cubs group has taught me about risk assessments and safeguarding children.'
- If you have a part-time job, such as in retail, remember those skills are transferable. Talk about working with the public, dealing with customer complaints and link to working with parents and carers.
- If you are older or have had a previous career do talk about the elements that you consider transferable. Career changers can offer a wide range of skills, be confident and showcase them.
- Sell yourself, sound passionate and committed!

Proofread – you need to be able to communicate with clarity.

Qualifications

You have to list your qualifications on the UCAS form, from GCSEs upwards; do access help or advice on this if you have international or unusual qualifications, from careers advice groups or your college/university advisors. All ITT is governed by Ofsted regulations and having Maths, English and Science GCSE or equivalent at C or grade 4 or higher is essential. Do check with your chosen providers what their entry requirements are. They should detail these on their own websites under entry requirements. Some providers accept equivalency tests, either from their own testing systems or external agencies, so if you do not have the core GCSES there may be other options. Certificates for GCSE and degrees will be requested for by all providers at interview, as it is an Ofsted requirement.

References

All providers will request that you provide at least one, probably two references. At least one of these should be from a school where you have worked or volunteered. The class teacher or a member of the leadership team should complete the reference and ensure that this refers to safeguarding and your suitability to work with children. If your other reference is from a workplace ask them to slant their reference towards working with children and schools, if possible. References are read by providers, so ensure they are truthful and showcase you at your best.

Skills tests

All primary and secondary teachers training in England have to pass two skills tests, one in Maths and one in English. No one can embark on ITT without having attained their skills tests. These are online tests that you book and sit in specific test centres around the country. You book separately for Maths and English. The English test has a focus on spelling, grammar and punctuation; if you have a diagnosis of certain special needs such as dyslexia you can be allowed extra time to complete the test. The Maths test requires answers within a timed sequence, so you need to be practised in quick fire mental maths skills. The first three tests are now free; after that you pay a fee. In January 2018 the rules were changed so that candidates can now sit the tests as many times as they need to. There are books, online revision guides, and many training providers also offer revision sessions too, so access help and support in order to have a successful start. We always recommend that candidates sit both tests soon after applying for ITT, and then use this as their baseline. If you pass, that's great, another job done; if not, then use the data to help you access support and revision. Avoid leaving the tests until the last minute, this puts far too much pressure on you and makes success less likely! See http://sta.education.gov.uk/

Other conditions

Everyone who works with children or vulnerable adults requires a Disclosure and Barring Service (DBS) check. Even if you have had one to work in schools, you will be required to complete an update or fill in a new form for your training year. This may be with your university or school provider depending on the route you have selected. These have to be completed before you start your training but you only fill them out once you know where you will be training, so you only do these once. If anything is revealed by your DBS you may be called to a DBS panel to discuss your suitability in greater depth.

You also have to complete a health questionnaire for your chosen provider (which is confidential). If there are any potential problems that would prevent you from being an effective teacher of young children, you will have to meet with the occupational health team to see if you are suitable and to see what support may be required.

The interview

You have researched your routes, attended open days or events, written a great personal statement and revised for your skills tests... what next?

Assuming you have followed the advice within the chapter, you have submitted your three applications via UCAS. Then you wait. However, unlike undergraduate degree courses, the ITT applications have to be dealt with within a tighter time frame, so you should hear back within a week or two. You may receive an email invitation to interview, so ensure your email address on your application is working well and appropriate (no sxyred-head@gmail.com please!). Check your junk mail too, as some invitations do go straight there for some accounts (Hotmail can be problematic).

For most interviews to ITT these days there will be a 'teach' aspect. This could be a short observed teaching session to a class, a group of children or other adults. It is vital that you prepare thoroughly for this. Read all the guidance carefully, and do not hesitate to contact the provider for more information about group size or resources, for example. If you are teaching a group or a session do get advice from serving teachers, and remember that the interviewers are not looking for teachers. They are looking for those with the capacity to become teachers, with support, in nine months.

Always plan the session carefully, ensuring you have a very clear learning objective to start with. Whenever planning any teaching, start with the objective and let the activity come from that, not the other way around. If you do not know the age group exactly, the best thing to do is to have several plans and resources to extend or contract the learning. Think about behaviour management, plan to include praise, and possibly rewards such as stickers. Ensure you introduce yourself (always as Miss/Ms/Mrs/Mr, never first names, be professional). If you are reading a story, ensure the book is large enough and pitched at the right age phase ('The Gruffalo' is well pitched for Reception but not suited to Year 4). Make sure you have practised the book and noted any tricky or specific vocabulary. If you have planned an activity ensure you have resources to hand such as pencils, paper, crayons and avoid planning to use the interactive whiteboard, as this can be complicated and notoriously prone to glitches.

Checklist for interviews

- Read the email/attachment carefully; do not forget any aspect.
- Pitch the teaching carefully (if you are unsure of age phase, then plan for a range, to level up or down).
- Have a clear learning objective, do not just do a 'nice activity'. There has to be something to learn.
- Remember behaviour – stand up when they enter, own the space, organise them and introduce yourself formally.
- Rehearse everything. Have a plan.
- Be prepared to reflect afterwards and discuss what happened.

Tricky issues

Clothing can be controversial; consider conservative, smart clothing, but this does not necessarily involving buying a suit. We would recommend no jeans, nothing cropped and a professional look, so polished shoes and brushed, tidy hair. It is recommended to cover large tattoos and remove facial piercings. This is contentious and many parents and carers do have all of these things. However, primary school teaching remains traditional in outlook and you may feel it is better to gain your place then have that conversation.

Finally

So, you look the part, have planned your teaching session, taken advice from teachers and ensured that you are up to date with teaching news (read the *Times Educational Supplement* (TES) and look online, educational Twitter is a good source). What else?

There may be tests to assess your maths or English skills, group activities to assess your team work and communication skills and then an individual or group interview. Interview questions are not designed to catch candidates out but rather probe your reasons for wanting to teach and what experiences you have already gained. Teacher retention is a huge issue currently, so the provider will want to ensure that you have the resilience and commitment for the role. They will also want to make you aware of key issues such as behaviour management and safeguarding and to find out what your strengths and areas for development are. I recommend that all candidates have an awareness of the Teacher Standards that govern all ITT programmes and are the standards against which all trainees are judged (www.gov.uk/government/publications/teachers-standards). Looking at the EYFS documents and the current National Curriculum would be a sensible idea too.

Remember that interviews are also the candidates' chance to ask questions of the provider, so ensure you do not go home without asking your burning question.

Suggested questions to ask at interview

- How do placements work?
- Who will support me on my placements?
- Will I be observed regularly on placement?

- When are timetables published?
- How do you assess trainees?
- How far away are placements?
- Can we find our own placements?
- Can I have support with essay writing?
- Is parking available locally?
- How many of your trainees end up in teaching jobs locally?
- Describe a typical day when we are with you in university/training school
- What can I do now to help with my preparation?

Post interview

Hopefully, having been organised and well prepared, you will find out that you have been offered a place at one of your three choices. This may happen via a phone call, email or formally via UCAS Track. You have the option of waiting until all three of your providers make a decision, or you can decline the other options and formally accept your offer. All offers will be conditional as you have to pass your degree (if you do not have it already), produce any missing certificates and pass your Skills Tests, DBS and health assessment. Your provider may also add in extra conditions depending on your interview and experience in schools. Your provider will start to send out information and probably hold a meeting for all trainees over the summer, so the fun starts here!

What if I am unsuccessful?

You may want to seek some feedback from the provider concerned. An email is usually the preferred format for this. It is important to listen to feedback if offered, as it could significantly improve your chances of selection at your next interview. If you struggle with interview techniques, talk to a careers advisor or your 'critical friend' teacher for further advice. Many providers will recommend more school experience for those who are unsuccessful, so consider spending time in a different school context (smaller/larger/more diverse/different age phases) to widen your experience.

If teaching is really your passion and you are rejected, do not give up. Look honestly at your skills, knowledge and experience, and brush up. If, however the process makes you reconsider if teaching really is for you, then look more widely and explore all the other options available for someone with your skills.

For detailed advice on preparing for an interview consult the careers service and online resources available at your place of study. However, there are some simple ground rules worth remembering.

Before the interview

- Confirm attendance.
- Check location and necessary travel arrangements.
- Research the job and the organisation.
- Arrange a mock interview at your place of study to practise your answers.
- Think of examples which illustrate your skills, knowledge and experience.
- Be up to date with the latest developments in the sector.

On the day

- Arrive early.
- Smile and introduce yourself.
- Speak clearly and confidently.
- Maintain eye contact and be aware of your body language.
- Ask for clarification if you do not understand a question.
- Relate your answers to the post.
- Be enthusiastic.

After the interview

- Do not dwell on the negative.
- Write down any questions you remember to help you prepare for future interviews.
- If unsuccessful contact the employer, thank them for the opportunity and ask for feedback.

Additional reading

- www.prospects.ac.uk – job roles, example CVs, letters
- www.yorkshiregraduates.co.uk
- www.jobsgopublic.com
- www.bapt.info – British Association of Play Therapists
- www.lgjobs.com – local government careers
- www.nahps.org.uk – National Association of Hospital Play Staff
- www.thefrontline.org.uk – social work child protection recruiting
- www.gov.uk/step-up-to-social-work-information-for-applicants – social work recruiting
- www.policenow.org.uk – police graduate recruitment
- www.charity-works.co.uk/apply/Third sector/ – charity graduate programme – Charity Works

Conclusion

As a result of your extensive work based practice and your academic studies, you have many of the skills, competencies, knowledge and experience required by employers and on postgraduate programmes of study. Before applying, do your research, audit your skills and match them to those required by the employer or programme of study. When completing the application form and personal statement, align your skills to those considered essential, and demonstrate your enthusiasm for the job or course. Make use of the readily accessible online resources as identified in this chapter. Remember the careers service can provide invaluable advice, support and guidance at every stage of the process, from finding the right job or course, completing the application form and preparing for interview. If you are unsuccessful at the application or interview stage, ask for feedback and try again. Good luck and enjoy this next exciting phase of your lives.

References

Mindtools (2018) *Personal SWOT analysis: making the most of your talents and opportunities.* Available at: wwwmindtools.com/pages/article/newTMC_05_1.htm (accessed 5 January 2018).

Ogilvie, C. and Homan, G. (2012). Everybody wins? Using the workplace as an arena for learning. *Higher Education, Skills and Work-Based Learning,* 2 (2), 102–120. doi:http://dx.doi.org.libaccess.hud.ac.uk/10.1108/20423891211224595

Organisation for Economic Cooperation and Development (OECD) (2017). *Getting skills right: skills for jobs indicators.* Paris: OECD Publishing.

Targetjobs (2018) *Be on top of the basics: essential skills and competencies.* Available at: https://targetjobs.co.uk/careers-advice/skills-and-competencies/420732-be-on-top-of-the-basics-essential-skills-and-competencies (accessed 9 February 2018).

Index